PRISM QUARTERLY

Brought to you by:

In partnership with

Poets & Writers Literary Forum
of Springfield, Illinois

Published Quarterly
January, April, July, October

Volume 8, Numbers 3&4
Winter 2007
ISBN 978-1-933923-03-1
ISSN 1554-4737

Published by:
Daybreak Press

3360 Carman Ave
Springfield, IL 62703

In cooperation with:

    Poets & Writers Literary Forum of Springfield, IL
    P.O. Box 5666
    Springfield, IL 62705-5666

Publishing Editor: David Pitchford
Co-Editor: Siobhan
Speculative Fiction and Poetry Editor: Daniel E. Blackston
Cover Art: "Bodhisattva" by Siobhan
Cover Design: David Pitchford

© Copyright 2007 by Daybreak Press

All rights reserved
Copyright for works
Reverts to individual authors

Phone: 217-529-9244 (David)
Fax: 217-529-9246
Email: prism@daybreakpoetry.com
www.pwlf.com
www.daybreakpoetry.com

ISBN 13: 978-1-933923-03-1
ISSN 1554-4737

Contents

Once, I Wanted to be the Weatherman	Barbara Robinette	1
Beloved	Barbara Robinette	2
1999, Five Years Old	Barbara Robinette	3
Falling	Elizabeth Huck	4
Turning	Elizabeth Huck	6
Wheels	Elizabeth Huck	7
The Miller's Tale	Elizabeth Huck	8
Argument	Elizabeth Huck	9
How to Attract	Elizabeth Huck	10
The Hour	Elizabeth Huck	11
Curiouser and Curiouser	Elizabeth Huck	12
Former Phone Psychic . . .	Elizabeth Huck	13
2006 Dancing Galliard Awards		14
Rest Stop	Christina Lovin	15
Love Needs the Dark	Christina Lovin	16
Inheritance	Christina Lovin	17
Love Bite	Christina Lovin	18
Eclipse	Christina Lovin	19
Laundry Day	Ellen Saunders	20
Tea for Three	Ellen Saunders	21
The Hour of Dinah's Rape	Yakov Azriel	22
Mount St. Helens	Emily Burns	23

Outbound	Dan Wormhoudt	24
The Question	David J. Rothman	25
Family Picnic	Marilyn L. Taylor	26
Cover Letter	Marilyn L. Taylor	27
Self-Portrait as Eve	Debra Wierenga	28
Transfiguration at Tanglewood	Gretchen Fletcher	29
Poets' Obits	Gretchen Fletcher	30
Why Fo'?	Larry Lyall	31
Reduced Speed Ahead	Raud Kennedy	32
But First You Have to Love Yourself	Raud Kennedy	33
Bruised Fruit	Raud Kennedy	34
Picture Frame	Raud Kennedy	35
Holidays	Raud Kennedy	36
Windy Nights	Rudyard Cahill IV	37
Never Forget	Peter Lee	38
The Beauty That Drives Us Mad	Peter Lee	39
Reflections on Death	Judi O'Brien Anderson	40
Legacy	Patricia Wellingham-Jones	41
I Dreamt of the Wind	Tracy M Rogers	42
Spring Has Withered	Tracy M Rogers	43
Loss	David Landrum	44
Moth	David Landrum	45
Why Petrarch is Rolling in His Grave (Review)	R. David Skinner	46
Petrarch's Sour Grapes: for Judith Goldhaber	R. David Skinner	51

Marilyn Blowing the Shofar	Judith Goldhaber	52
The Hanging of Mary Surratt	Richard Fein	53
Pistachio Cravings	Anita Stienstra	54
Drawn in Light	Anita Stienstra	55
Life Imitates Life	Anita Stienstra	56
I Fell Beside an Ocean	David M. Pitchford	57
Love and Longing on the Loop	Bud Bartlett	58
Ten Ways to Knock the Block	David M. Pitchford	67
Memory Drills	Robert Cooperman	77
Cora Myers . . . American Legion Hall	Robert Cooperman	78
Mike Gooden . . . American Legion Hall	Robert Cooperman	79
Like it or Not	C. L. Gunther	80
An Image of Us	C. L. Gunther	81
Wedge	C. L. Gunther	82
Sitting by a Lake in Las Vegas, NM	John Dean	83
Molly Sings for the Ward	Hugh Jones	84
Go by Art's	Hugh Jones	85
Death Wish	May Kinsolving	86
The Garrulous Man	May Kinsolving	88
Ono no Komachi	May Kinsolving	89
The Female Horseshoe Crab	Graham Duncan	90
Going On	Graham Duncan	91
The Bard's Words	Graham Duncan	92
You, Anne Sexton	Danielle Minzenberger	93

Road Hike	Ken Sibley	94
Forgotten Country	David Radavich	95
Casualties	David Radavich	96
Hate-Speech	David Radavich	97
Odysseus When Young	E. G. Burrows	98
Centipedes	E. G. Burrows	99
Crime Solution	E. G. Burrows	100
Miniature	Fillmore Lewis	101
How Much	William Meyer	102
When Shadows Fall	William Meyer	103
AP's Person Without	William Meyer	104
A Glass of Heads	William Meyer	105
Foul	Peter Layton	106
Aspects	Peter Layton	107
After	Peter Layton	108
The Big Boys	Jamie Mauldin	109
Business Trip Blues	Jamie Mauldin	110
Things I Have Learned	Karen R. Porter	111
Quarrelers	Arthur Gottlieb	112
Getting Over It	Arthur Gottlieb	113
The High Ground	Ed Galing	114
The Answer	Ed Galing	116
Waiting to be Weaned	Shari Koopmann	117
Antaeus	Shari Koopmann	118

Arborglyphs	Thomas Robert Barnes	120
A Prioir	Thomas Robert Barnes	121
Twains	Thomas Robert Barnes	122
Blue October Light	J. R. Campbell	123
The Path Gains Its Agent	Travis Delaware	124
Fiddling with My Life	Siobhan	135
Mascara Stains	Siobhan	136
I Picture Crows	Siobhan	137
Affair of the Dark	David M Pitchford	138
Down to the River, Pray	David M Pitchford	141
Oh, My Sisters	Marcellus Leonard	142
Dust Angels	R. David Skinner	145
Bargeman's Castles in the Sand	TC Baylor	146
Bodhisattva: Eighth Chakra	R David Skinner	153
The Home	Joe Kreisberg	154
3 Sonnet Dialogues	Siobhan & David M Pitchford	160
Victory at Xandr-Din	David M Pitchford	167
Usurper	David M Pitchford	184
The GATES of ARCADIA		186
Dragons Over Sunset Island	James Princeton Garr	188
Utopian Moon Waning	Fillmore Lewis	193
Azieran: Brotherhood of Rot	Christopher Heath	194
The Sun or the Moon	Cheryl Peugh	205
Changeling	Edward J. McFadden III	216
Dark Leviticus	Nathan Meyer	222

WELCOME

WOW! Amazing how far one can get behind with all this life going on around us. My humblest apologies for the lateness of this publication. I make no excuses, yet ask your indulgence.

Since beginning this issue, I have taken on numerous other responsibilities as well as facing the myriad challenges a small publisher faces.

In December 2006 it was my great honor to accept the position of Museum Editor for the Illinois State Museum. I love the position immensely and intend to continue there until forcibly removed (retired or fired). Editing tasks at the Museum have kept me quite busy for the intervening time, as I came into that position up against deadlines with two quarterly publications, which, ironically, are also double issues meant to catch up on schedules, deadlines, etc. So it will be a great relief to have these three projects closed and the next issues under way.

One of the wonderful side effects of having this current issue of *Prism* still open is that we have the opportunity to include the announcement and winning entries of the 2006 Dancing Galliard Sonnet Contest. This year's contest was a beast to judge—we had excellent response, and all the sonnets, save maybe two, are, in my estimation, worthy to publish. The prizes were decided by photo-finish as it were, and ultimately had to be decided by the Chair of the prize committee.

Some details of the journal's continuation are still to be worked out as parts of the editing staff have since resigned. However, as publishing editor and creator of this journal, I assure you that it will continue as long as I have the ability to continue publishing.

We start off again with the wonderful verses of Barbara Robinette and follow those with a special feature of poems by Elizabeth Huck, who succeeded me as president of the Poets & Writers Literary Forum of Springfield, Illinois. Her poetic skill is clearly evident in the sampling of poems herein presented. Following that feature is the announcement of the 2006 Dancing Galliard Sonnet Contest winners, and then winning entries. Again, I am very grateful to Dr. Robert Seufert and Judith Goldhaber for their willingness and diligence in serving on the awards committee. Also, as ever, I am grateful to Ethan Lewis and Corrine Frisch for their time, attention, and wine. My undying gratitude to this journal's co-editor, Siobhan, for her administrative support as well as her ongoing moral support, stalwart reinforcement, and editorial input.

This issue is packed. We have a wonderful array of talent from newcomers as well as returning contributors. Raud Kennedy is quickly becoming a PQ staple, as are Tracy Rogers and Bud Bartlett. It is a pleasure to see more poetry again from Anita Stienstra, a central Illinois poet whom I consider among the most talented and skilled among us. It's a special treat for me to see so many Davids gracing our pages, as well as seeing new names and new approaches by first-time contributors.

This issue will be the last containing the "Gates of Arcadia" section, as Mr. Blackston has resigned all positions relating to this journal. This does not signify by any means that *Prism* will discontinue including speculative fiction and poetry; it merely means that all such content will go through the general submission procedures. An evolutionary title is being considered for that section, and we are certainly hopeful of hearing from our readers and contributors on the matter.

We hope you enjoy the read!

David Pitchford
February 2007

We welcome your comments and invite your feedback:
David Pitchford
3360 Carman Ave
Springfield, IL 62703

Fax: 217-529-9246

Email: davidpitchford@daybreakpoetry.com

ONCE, I WANTED TO BE THE WEATHERMAN

I saw a sky that took me back to long ago.
Its coat was gray and calm its look to third grade thought.
Then I gazed into the gentle frown my teacher gave
these dreaming eyes.
My hope to be the weather man
put on her coat to stand in line...
for outside games and empty swings
on a playground gone.

Barbara Robinette

BELOVED

Are poetry and I sisters in
the back seat?
Then who is driving in
 the front seat?
And as we clutch each
other in merry
glee, bumping gaily
over cobbled roads,
tall trees casting shadows long,
do we think, *do we think,*
"where did *she* come from?"

Barbara Robinette

1999, Five Years Old

We walked down the city's hot sticky
sidewalk. Blaring car
horns, smelly bus fumes.
Mommy.
Daddy.
And me
you held my hand
so tight
your knuckles big and white.
Were you mad at me?

I kept fidgeting widgeting and finally
broke away . . .
Anyway . . .
And so today
I skipped lightly atop a little
grassy knoll by the parking lot.

Puffy white dandelions crowned my mound.
I stood tall waving to wispy
clouds drifting by. Cool, dark
trees beckoned
with playful shade down
the red bricked street

and you, hunched over,
smoked a cigarette and
counted your change.

Barbara Robinette

Falling

It began falling in the night. It woke no one, made no sound, broke no sleep.

The radio clicked on, assembling the day out of music and news, scattering Dora's dreams. She opened her eyes, saw today's suit laid out on its chair, closed her eyes, burrowed into the pillow.

A snarl cut through the upbeat vocals, the snarl of a plow. Dora turned over, listened past the music to the traffic. Traffic passing with a whisper, not with a roar. She climbed out of bed, groped with her feet for slippers, crossed to the window and raised the blind.

Yes. Already it covered the grass, piled against the house almost to the sill, and still it fell. Like sheets of gauze swaddling the eyes of a patient after surgery.

In her mind she heard the scrape, scrape of the shovel against asphalt, felt the weight pulling down the muscles of her arms, her shoulders, her back.

She jerked the cord to lower the blind; it cracked against the sill. First things first. Shower. Breakfast. Maybe it will go away. Turn to rain. Maybe they'll close the state offices. Ha.

Beyond the kitchen window, the back yard waited, sheeted like an abandoned room. White-draped bulks against white gloom, blurred outlines of rosebushes, hedges, patio furniture, a bird feeder. The branches of the great Douglas fir dripped with cold cobwebs.

Dora tied her flannel robe tighter, filled the kettle, took oat bread and a pink grapefruit from the refrigerator. The radio chanted a roster of school closings. Why didn't they just say what was open, it would take a lot less time. The blade of the chopping knife mirrored the bulb over the counter, white circles running up and down the carbon steel.

Back in her bedroom, Dora pried two slats of the blinds apart. Muffled headlights ghosted past, glimpsed and smothered. She turned from the window. The navy skirt and jacket waited, draped over the chair, beside the neat black pumps and the Executive Carryall.

In two strides, she reached the bedside phone. She punched buttons, spoke without hesitation or apology, replaced the phone, and climbed back into bed. Pulled up the comforter. Snuggled into the pillow. Closed her eyes.

The snow kept falling.

Elizabeth Huck

Turning

"Turn the page, Daddy."

"I'm not finished with this page yet."

"Turn it anyway."

"Why?"

"I want to see the picture. It's on the next page."

"Look, do you want me to read to you or not?"

"I know the stupid story. I want to see the picture! The purple horse on the merry-go-round, and the moon. And the silver leopard."

Also the sky-blue dolphin, and the pink and green snake. The carousel turns under the moon. Golden lights. Bright calliope music playing. Long golden fringe on the canopy.

She can't see the animals on the other side of the carousel, there is only the one picture. Sometimes she imagines there is nothing on the other side, only these four creatures she knows and loves. Sometimes she imagines something wonderful on the other side, a splendid dragon or lordly lion or a princess' coach. But more often she thinks it is a terrible monster, locked in the same circle with the beautiful animals. It keeps them prisoner, or maybe it's the other way round.

The story doesn't tell her, the carousel isn't important in it, just a picture of an amusement park the children in the book get lost in one night. She thinks the children in the book are stupid, and doesn't care about them.

Daddy has a copy of the picture made for her as a birthday present. Framed and hung on her wall, over the bed. It makes her uncomfortable; she sleeps, now, with the book under her pillow, holding it tight, while the moon crosses the sky and the hands of the bedside clock turn round and round.

Elizabeth Huck

WHEELS

In a garden at June's ending, long evening
hours stretch thin as the sky, the wide sky where sight
runs out to infinity, stretch to the point
of breaking, to the moment at the wheel's top, where the child
hangs, in the illusion of motion halted, of a moment
sealed in glass, or as in the gondola
of a balloon, caught in hard blue, feeling no movement
while distant lawns and fields and the roads
that mark them are shifting their angles, degree
by imperceptible degree, as the sun shifts, until the shadow
of the balloon rides the cornfields, as light
dissolves, as colors deepen into truth before dark
back in the garden, where firefly candles flash,
momently, in the kindled present, in the now
flaring and gone within the glass forever.

Elizabeth Huck

THE MILLER'S TALE

I'd forgotten what the land was like
on a February morning, this emptiness,
scattered lines of snow dribbled onto blank
brown pages, open left and right from the gray
spine of the highway. I'm moving through
a slow story, no rush, take your time, savor
the description, the details. Notice
white mist at the horizon, thinning
into clear gray, the angle
power lines cut across the sky. Action
will catch up soon enough, don't
hurry it on, let them pass, gunning
their engines and zipping by, no space for more
than a glance, no contact
between eye and eye. Let it unfold
at its own pace, the green mile posts
counting down leisurely to zero, to the point
of memory, of lost tales retold.

Elizabeth Huck

ARGUMENT

I am too old
to play in leaves. I will
rake them properly
into neat piles, ready
for the long row of yard bags,
stuffed, silent and brown
as the bare branches. I will not
drop to my knees in this crunchy
heap of yellow and red,
toss handfuls in the air like confetti,
and I will certainly not
lie down and roll
over and over
laughing like a child
on a long weekend,
nor walk my grownup road
with wine-colored scraps
clinging to my hair.

Elizabeth Huck

How to Attract

How to attract the pigeon:
don't.
She comes of herself,
drives off the wanted,
the small painted singers
for which you build houses,
choose premium seed mix,
baffle the squirrels.
Not for these rippling buff feathers,
this plump smooth
creamy body and iridescent
head. Beauty wouldn't come
without asking, make its own nests
on our awnings and chimneys.
Treasure would not give itself
unearned.

Elizabeth Huck

THE HOUR

A closed circle
of photographs
pasted together like a clock

hangs

above my father's bed,
above abandoned cane
and wheeled chair.

Counting from the top,
the scarce, early scenes—
    the faded boy-face
    that mirrors my brother's;
    the young man in uniform;
    the black-and-white wedding.

Children and color
arrive about five o'clock;
a crowded collage—
houses and jobs,
pets and pleasures—
swings up the west side
    to the first grandchild
    at the top,
    at noon
    or midnight,
    at the stroke of the hour.

Noticed by all
who stop to visit
and look for words,
it waits
framed and finished.

Elizabeth Huck

Curiouser and Curiouser

Your questions pluck at my illusions
like fingers stripping the vine
that wraps around the porch rail,
pulling and tugging,
ripping one section free,
leaving a length of fluttering leaves
still clinging to wrought iron,
not yet knowing itself
torn from its root.

Elizabeth Huck

A Phone Psychic Describes Her Job to Her Former Welfare Worker

I'm telling you, the soaps
got nothing on these stories
people tell me every day, and I'm even
paid to listen. Always the same
question—I'm lonely, I'm broke, my kids
are going to hell, I'm sick, nobody knows me, nobody
cares, how do I get
out? That's what they want, all of them, the way
out, Prince Charming, the lottery, Lana Turner
in the drugstore. The lightning strike, the tornado
blowing Kansas away for good.

       I follow the script,
tell them what I'm paid
to say, what they need to hear. You'll make it,
baby, everything's lining up, love,
money, health, fame,
I see it coming for you, just
grab the moment, the planets
are on your side. You'd think
the poor bitches could see, you wouldn't figure
I could get away with this, but they
keep coming back.

       Funny.
You'd of cut me off,
snap, if I lied like that
on your forms, but lying
is my job now, and they keep calling. Somehow
it's true for them.

Elizabeth Huck

Daybreak Press Proudly Announces Its 2006 Dancing Galliard Sonnet Contest Winners:

Grand Prize: Christina Lovin

Galliard Sonneteer: Ellen Saunders
for "Laundry Day"
with Honorable Mention for "Tea for Three"

Journeyman: Yakov Azriel for "The Hour of Dinah's Rape"
with Honorable Mention for his sonnet cycle

Honorable Mentions:

Emily Burns: "Mount St. Helens"

Dan Wormhoudt: "Outbound"

David J. Rothman: "The Question"

Marilyn L. Taylor: "Family Picnic"
& "Cover Letter"

Debra Wierenga: "Self-Portrait as Eve"

Gretchen Fletcher: "Poets' Obits"
& "Transfiguration at Tanglewood"

All prizes and certificates were awarded in February 2007.
Watch www.prismquarterly.com/contest.htm
for further contest announcements.

REST STOP

I phoned because I wanted him to know
that I was going to be gone for just
a day or two (for he might worry). So,
I made the call. His voice draws tense across
the mapped and measured emptiness between
that junction (where my turning right had left
him stalled before the light that never greened,
but flashed bright caution over signs that read:
"No Turns," "Dead End") and here, where pavements stretch
away, and I have pulled aside to call.

I wave off flies that rise from empty flesh—
it rots beside the road. *My cup is full.*
"I bought two Playboys." Pause. "*The coffee steams.*
"It's not the same," he says. *I add more cream.*

Christina Lovin

LOVE NEEDS THE DARK

The strongest bloom cannot endure the sun
without relief of cloud or shade or night.
For even cactus blossoms come undone

if not for respite from the burning sun.
The life that waits inside the scattered seed
is scorched when cast in its uncovered plight

and dies, save for the somber soil of need,
the evening dews. Love needs the dark to grow
as well it seems—like any other weed

would stretch its face toward the brightest glow
of light to find its stalk drawn thin and feet
unsteady in the soil. Desire to know

me then in blackest moods, in rage, defeat,
and learn: *without the dark love dies,* my sweet.

Christina Lovin

INHERITANCE

I eat the food my mother cooks and serves.
At ninety-three, she waits on me and death
with equal patience and expenditure
of energy, measuring out the breadth
and height of every breath. Her days slice thin
as apples for the pies she knows by heart:
the spices stale within the dusty tins,
that pinch of salt that livens flour and lard,
shrunken fruit as wizened as her face,
the circle that she rolls without a tear
and mothers into her mother's granite plate.
Her table, like her life now, is small and square.

Her shuddering blade divides the weeping pie—
the lacerated pastry seeps and sighs.

Christina Lovin

"Inheritance" was previously published by Finishing Line Press in Christina's chapbook *What We Burned for Warmth* as well as in the anthology *Susan B & Me*.

LOVE BITE

"A pinch," she claims. Then, glances down to where
two stigma, like an exclamation point,
have spread their shame into the shoulder
flesh, so tender where the arm and torso join.
She shifts the straps of bag and bra apart
as if to prove mechanics of the injury:
the perjured witness of that biting smart
of teeth: sweet suck between the lips of sigh
and moan, and blood that stains like when the moon
has pulled the salt sea higher inch by inch
then slips away to leave the shorelines strewn
with evidence. She swears, "It's just a pinch,"
(that pervading proof of passion's purple art)
and lays her hand across her liar's heart.

Christina Lovin

ECLIPSE

Face raised to darkening moon—a twilight sky
due to the shadowed sun—small crescent burned
into the unlit mirror of the eye

recalls to me a childhood lesson learned
too late: *Don't look! Don't look!* My mother's hand
a brand against my cheek, my father's stern

and searing glare, his voice a hot command.
And that dark heat that surges from your eyes:
the deadly light, coronas that expand

around the shield you raise between us. Wise,
a woman turns away but I mistook
for passion what would come to cauterize

my innocence and leave a scar. I shook
myself, demanding this: *Don't look! Don't look!*

Christina Lovin

LAUNDRY DAY

When Mondays break with morning sky as clear
and blue and wide as were my mother's eyes,
I think about the times when I would hear
the screen door slam, then hear her pensive sighs.
How piece by piece she picked and snapped the clothes
she stretched and pinned across the line to slap
the sky like sails let loose in wind. Lord knows
how they were tied within a mother's trap
so tightly wound no storm could break the hold
and set them free. One winter day she tried
to leave them there to stiffen in the cold,
as if some dream inside of her had died.
But evening came and in her flannel gown
she walked outside and took the laundry down.

Ellen Saunders

TEA FOR THREE

My two dolls sit in wicker chairs and take
their tea from cups and plates with rims of pink
with crust-less sandwiches and fancy cake,
at which they stare with eyes that never blink.
It seems to be a perfect way to pass
an afternoon, while dressed in lace with socks
of silk. Their hats have bows as green as grass
with little flowers, and perch upon locks
of curly, yellow hair. To think that they
will never have a worry or a thought,
or know how things can change from day to day,
or whether it is cold or very hot.
If I am ever missing, you might see
a little table set with tea for three.

Ellen Saunders

The Hour of Dinah's Rape

> *"Dinah, the daughter of Leah whom she had borne to Jacob, went out to see the daughters of the land. When Shechem, the son of Hamor the Hivite, the prince of the land, saw her, he took her, lay with her by force, and violated her." — (Genesis 34:1-2)*

This is the hour when Temple gates are burned,
when altars are profaned, when Temple priests
become the sacrifice instead of beasts;
this is the hour for which the rapist yearned.
        This is the hour when heaven is overturned,
        when sunsets in the west are now the east's
        last hope of light, as darkness eats its feast;
        this is the hour when all her pleas are spurned.

This is the hour when hours are scorched to death
and time itself is buried under sod;
the present has no life, the past—no power
        to move its limbs, the future has no breath,
        when all she sees is the hidden face of God.
        This is the month, week, day. This is the hour.

Yakov Azriel

MOUNT ST. HELENS

A crouching, headless, jagged-throated beast,
brindled black and white with ash and snow,
looms above the forest to the east.
It blew itself apart some years ago.

The mountain steams into the clear blue air
and builds its dome; the ridges that it gnawed
with avalanches still are mostly bare.
The silence is profound—the air, still awed.

The rivers flow away, their valleys green,
their floodplains full of thick volcanic mud.
Splintered stumps remain. This place has seen
a blasted wood, a steaming, roiling flood.

Perhaps God reaches down when no-one sees
and strokes the healing land's soft pelt of trees.

Emily Burns

Outbound

Seeping into the concourse through slits of glass,
daylight collects like green water in a tank,
suspending us. He talks to make time pass,
I stall for it. "Tickets, money—don't thank
us you earned it, change planes in Norita, write."
He goes, each step a multiple in miles
from home, walking then running for the Bangkok flight.
The girl who waits there, sure he'll make it, smiles.

The girl will vanish out on the China Sea,
fever nearly kill him, alone in Beijing.
One comrade will rob him over Russian tea,
another buy him fries in a Moscow Burger King.
Starting out, how could either of us know
the distance, boy to man, he'd have to go?

Dan Wormhoudt

THE QUESTION

"Doc," I said, "it's so confusing now.
My life . . . my family . . . I can't make sense . . ."
He stopped, looked up, all ears, a furrowed brow.
I went on. Had to. The pressure so immense,
words spilling out. "I mean, I'm 46,
and all my dreams, I don't . . ." Took a deep breath.
No good. Began to cry. "I just can't fix . . ."
Sob, " . . . Anything, and so afraid of death . . .
So many things I never meant to say . . .
Mistakes, I mean . . . and all the loneliness . . ."
Regained control and tried to laugh. "Hey,
not to mention the world's a total mess . . ."
X-rays in hand, puzzled, he said "I see . . .
But aren't you here to talk about your knee . . ?"

David J. Rothman

Family Picnic

Life hasn't been easy for Betsy since she turned
thirteen—just look at her, the sniffy way
she sits all by herself, wincing with scorn
at her noisy cousins lining up to play
a pick-up softball game before the day
runs out. *Childish*, she mutters from the chair
in which she lounges, tossing back her hair.

But now, two uncles and a favorite aunt
are filling in at right field and third base;
Betsy's breathing quickens, but she can't
stop buffing her nails, sucking in her face,
keeping her careful distance—just in case
we take her for that splendid child *Betsy*,
who left us only very recently.

Marilyn L. Taylor

COVER LETTER

Dear Sir or Madam: In this envelope
please find some poems that I have written.
I send them to you in the earnest hope
that you will read them and be wildly smitten.
In fact, you'll jump up, cheering, from your chair
and holler out, *Hey, get a load of these!*
We've got the poems of the decade here,
we'd better print them in our journal! Jeez,
is this a little miracle, or what?
And then you'll fax or phone me right away
to tell me that you're breaking out a split
of Taittinger, to toast your lucky day
and call me back to say you might as well
FedEx my check this minute, what the hell.

Marilyn L. Taylor

SELF-PORTRAIT AS EVE

I never use a peeler. I prefer
the *frisson* of a paring knife
chasing my thumb around the equator
of a red-green globe. I'm a risk-starved wife,
peeling apples for a son who insists
on naked fruit. I eat a snakey coil of skin
and he says I'm disgusting, then kisses
me on the mouth.

                                      I'd do it again—
marry the man, carry the sons, I'd eat
the whole McIntosh, seeds and all.
But I keep an eye peeled for that serpent.
I'm yearning for another Fall
and watching for new fruit to grow—
there's something else I need to know.

                            Debra Wierenga

TRANSFIGURATION AT TANGLEWOOD

Ozawa's mighty arms spread out like wings
to bring a symphony across the lawn.
The orchestra's broad brass and sustained strings
fling out gold stars that light the sky like dawn.
The Mahler echoes out across the hills
and drops like rain from Berkshires' massive pines
down on my ears until my whole soul fills
and makes me feel as drunk as though from wine.
Our picnics packed so carefully lie shut
lest opening them would break the music's spell,
and stop the train of Mahler's powerful thought.
While in my ear the music starts to swell
like a balloon too large for me to hold.
It bursts and I become those stars of gold.

Gretchen Fletcher

Poet's Obits

So often in the *N.Y. Times* obits
I've read some out-of-context, virguled lines
buried in stories of the lives and works of poets
who've died and left a lot of words behind
like bread crumbs on the forest floor for us
to follow. I have gathered up my share
and felt lucky as some wealthy heiress
who's willed a whole estate from God knows where—
out of the blue. I've used each polished gem
of poetry they've left behind and tried
out poems of my own inspired by them,
for which I thank those poets who have died.
I wonder: Which of my lines will they quote?
Or will it even say in my obit, "She wrote"?

Gretchen Fletcher

WHY FO'?

Why fo' dat bitch Katrina she don whump
& stomp & howl dat she bring down de house,
uproot de flo', & den uprear de swamp,
den tro' dem on de roof dem kids, de spouse,
den tron' my sweet coon ass rat top dat tree
rat by dat street dat ain't no street no mo',
down where dem niggahs floats dey boat, ongree,
& counts dey dead what never had wha' fo'
to git & go? Why fo' dem empty suits
what on tv dey mou't dem pretty words
den not wit shit do dem what rapes & loots,
'dem what's sick & damn near drown?—Dem turds!

& what's wit dis: dem folks what say de Prez
don' tak a "fly-by," den haul ass-dat Whizz!?

Larry Lyall

REDUCED SPEED AHEAD

His bottle of e.d. pills rolls across the dash
as they speed through the turn
in his new red Porsche.
His heavy 'girlfriend' has frosted hair
instead of gray.
Middle age is a washed out memory
in the rear view mirror
as the Grim Reaper
leans over the backs of their seats
and glances at their speed.

Raud Kennedy

But First You Have to Love Yourself

Maybe moving back to the town
I grew up in was a complete mistake,
just chasing twenty year old ghosts.
When I left, everyone was older than me.
Now I'm one of them. The old.
Gray beard, anonymous pains that find
a new spot to warm each morning.
When I last lived here I was a punk,
and if that punk sat
next to my current self,
he'd smirk and chuckle,
not recognizing himself.
And I'd grumble about sitting
next to a know nothing
dolt.

Raud Kennedy

BRUISED FRUIT

The fragility of our bodies
goes forgotten until injured.
A deep cut, a broken bone,
and then the healing.
Can a smile repair
a sneer's damage?
Fragility is the common
Denominator.
Even steel melts.
Planets die, suns implode,
and we are as gnats
on a floating plum.

Raud Kennedy

PICTURE FRAME

Reflections in the mirror
don't leave stains
like a cut on the face
leaves a scar.
Torn tissue never to return
as it was.
Pedaling my bicycle
through my errors.
Of judgment, choices.
Who is my friend.
Who isn't.

Raud Kennedy

HOLIDAYS

Today
is one of those days
where,
no matter how nice or kind,
everyone
will make me sick.
Grandmothers
coddling their grand kids,
dog walkers and Samaritans,
whistling,
people who press the walk button,
and don't wait
should be put in stocks.
Same goes for people
who fidget, stuff their faces,
and read newspapers loudly.
I'm exhausted,
wiped out from yesterday.
Who knew
forcing conversation with people
I see twice a year
could sap
so much life.

Raud Kennedy

WINDY NIGHTS

the dog howls unreason
midwestern gales
sweep through—
who will sweep up after?

night billows in on quilted fronts
swears tornadoes
threatens lightnings
cusses in thunder-chorus
    THE CRADLE WILL ROCK

birds tremble in tree hollows
flick feathers like a middle-age man
sheds hairs in his shower
worried over—
what passes in the night . . . .

Rudyard Cahill IV

NEVER FORGET

With two steel prongs, three and
a half inches apart—long, sharp,

like those of a fork you'd
use to feed a whole chicken

to a croc, or maybe roast
a pair of foot-long hot dogs—

it shone behind glass in the
"Museum of Applied Art"
in Belgrade in the early 1990s,

had been employed by the Croats
hundreds of years ago to gouge

out two Serb eyeballs at a time—
little different than the repeated

name of a gunned-down brother
when Crips are going for Blood
(or vice versa)—an old instrument

with a new use: to justify
the rape, torture, starvation,

and/or murder of more than one
million Muslims in Christ's name.

How far does our memory reach?
Does it stretch beyond tall towers,

or end at the points
of two steel prongs?

Peter Lee

The Beauty that Drives Us Mad

the beauty that drives us mad
is found not only in the eyes
and hair of a magnificent girl
but in two ants pulling an apple seed
in opposing directions it is found

in the wheel of a common pigeon
above a strip mall and in the smoke
from a freight truck clearing its head
beauty is found in death and therefore
old men invite young men to war

beauty is what we refuse to see
as we struggle for safer lives
after all the suburban tracts
are crowded with blind seers
sharing walls in cul-de-sacs

beauty leaves us unsheltered unprepared
we climb onto the rooftops to shout it
to the world and are there struck dumb
for the rest of our lives by the beauty
that words cannot describe

so it is that we return to ground
to stare silently at our feet
until it becomes unbearable
then we stare up at the sky
until that becomes unbearable too

and that's when we go mad
or we go blind.

Peter Lee

Reflections on Death

Reflection #1

How long has it been
since that night
when we,
young and indestructible
held each other
united against the world?

Reflection on One Dying

I thought I saw
a breath of summer
touch your eyes
before the shutters fell.

To Kurt

Don't you know the sun and I
had to break horizon
without you this morning?

You buried inspiration and youth.
You left debts unpaid, songs unplayed.
Suicide leaves metallic mourning.

Sweet Seduction

When Death extends her invitation
my heart flutters
in fine-honed calligraphy.

Sweet seduction

Rainbow colors string my vision
caress my breath, and
settle coppery on my tongue.

Judi O'Brien Anderson

LEGACY

From winter quarters after Bull Run
he writes on paper flimsy as his hopes
to his beloved Becky, five years old
and safe at home.

Through firing lines and bivouacs,
by horseback and hand to hand,
the letter travels stained
with a father's exhausted tears.

A few letters finally arrive,
are pored over, carried in pockets,
no substitute for the father
who died of his wounds.

A hundred and forty years later
I finger those fragile bits of paper,
squint to decipher the faded script,
feel the longing in each line.

I thank my ancestors who saved
the few creased and torn pages
from a Civil War battlefield
for a great-great-granddaughter
with grandchildren of her own.

Patricia Wellingham-Jones

I Dreamt of the Wind

I dreamt of the wind blowing carelessly through my hair
and tangling the fine feathers as they intertwine
turning the leaves inside out and exposing their tender undersides
to signal the coming of the summer storm

I dreamt of the wind on my grandma's porch in the summertime
making the springs on the old porch swing creak and sigh
touching my face and arms with its soft hands
and cooling the sweltering summer air

I dreamt of the wind in the lush valley below where you lay
rustling the autumn leaves and carrying the call of the old church house
sighing and waiting for the day they brought you home
to carry a fine silt of red clay from your lonely grave

I dreamt to the wind through the old tulip tree
kissing the faces of the pale pink blooms I once brought you
breaking the brittle brown limbs and scattering them on the ground
where the tall grass dances around their corpses

I dreamt of the wind against my window at night
moaning mournfully and longing for daybreak, as I long for you,
tapping against the shutters and settling the bricks
until daylight returns to warm its icy fingers.

Tracy M. Rogers

Spring Has Withered . . .

Spring has withered on the vine,
bleached and scattered to the fiery wind
beneath the scalding summer sun,
like the lilacs that bloomed not so long ago,
their delicate lavender petals flourished
and faded much too soon.

And, high atop the sycamore tree
the bluebird no longer sings —
He has fled the summer swelter
on a temperate Northeastern breeze,
only to return for December's wintry haze.

Oh, what is to be done for those who languish
withering beneath the sultry summer sun,
who find no respite in the moon's tepid luster
or the gentle sway of sycamore leaves?
No fervent repentance, no cheap grace
shall rescue us from this scorching inferno.

Tracy M. Rogers

Loss

Nauplion, Greece, 2004

I left my passport in Crete,
my sandals in a cheap hotel in Athens,
my pleasing ways somewhere near Epidurus.

The vistas I saw from Acro-Corinth,
the painful loveliness of the Samaria Gorge,
cancelled longing for this or that.
I grew content to lose—here, where losing is a way of life.

David W. Landrum

MOTH

The first mistake was yours.
You flew toward what you thought was light, circling, bumping walls,
thumping out the window then back in.

I touched you, unaware your wings were wet.
You had only just emerged,
beautifully scarred, from a twenty-year cocoon.

My fingertips (I thought them gentle)
leeched your moist life
into their parchment,
hindered your unfolding flight.

I kept you safe from spider webs
set treacherously in spaces
where the moon is dim;
gave you sanctuary from lepidopterists
who would have impaled and encased
your curious beauty.

But the scars I made on you will never heal.
Your wings bear alien patterns.
My fingerprints are molded to your flight.

David W. Landrum

Why Petrarch is Rolling in His Grave:
A Review of Judith Goldhaber's *Sonnets from Aesop*

You have to love the sensationalist title my editor stuck me with—okay, so he merely suggested it **strongly**. On the other hand, what's *not* to like about Aesop? Isn't it time someone found an innovative way to revive love for and interest in this lion of the literary age of classics? How brilliant an idea is it to kill both proverbial birds with one stone and do the reintroduction via poetry? Brilliant! Petrarch is rolling in his grave because he didn't think to do it in the sonnet—it was someone's else genius.

With that introduction, I suppose you're ready to hear that the sonnets in Goldhaber's book are primarily Petrarchan. They are not. Well, unless you're much more lenient than Clement Wood, whose crash course in verse opens Random House's *Complete Rhyming Dictionary*. Purists have much to roll in their graves over, or merely roll their eyes at, and those of us in the Pope school smile, chortling inside, and herald a new addition to the American, if not the Western, Canon. These poems are primarily a common variation of the Petrarchan with a rhyme scheme of A-B-B-A-A-B-B-A-C-D-D-C-E-E sans stanza breaks—effectively creating a stichic verse of what many consider a stanzaic classical form. One could classify the verse in this collection as a Neo Classic deviation from the Petrarchan sonnet, or at least the majority of the verses that carry the above stated rhyme scheme. There are numerous other schema, but let's skip the dry Constructionist rhetoric and get on with the review. . .

Revivalist efforts are somewhat an academic standard—mimesis demands that we model our craft after the masters of the past. But still, there seems to be a dearth of recent projects with true merit as far as I have seen. Goldhaber's project, though, strikes me as a masterpiece concept—a once in a lifetime stroke of genius.

This of course raises the question of whether the book lives up to the brilliance of its concept. Does it? Well . . . perhaps it would be disrespectful of me to offer a conclusion on the matter, so I'll deal here with the evidence and let the jury decide. We'll start by pointing out some of the parts of the work that could be touched up to polish the collection into Greek marble perfection. Then I'll deal with the perfections already extant, and point out some of the *flaws* that mark *Sonnets from Aesop* as a masterpiece.

In a world that eschews rigidity in its poetic forms, what does it take to make a sonnet? I vacillate, personally, between quasi-rigid adherence to the sonnet as outlined in *The New Princeton Encyclopedia of Poetry and Poetics* and a sort of 14-line free-for-all sonnet conception (opposing 'form' or 'formula'). In the neoclassic vein, I pretty much decide if a verse is a sonnet by whether it works as a sonnet. By that stricture, I have serious reservations considering some of the verses in this collection as sonnets. Goldhaber in at least 14 instances has more than fourteen lines.

Most noticeable is "The Man, the Boy, and the Donkey," which finishes out the collection with an 18-line verse. Ironically (hysterically funny as well), this poem serves, via its moral of "please all, please none," as a sort of warning against this very activity of criticism, or at least warns the critic that the poet has no need to heed such criticism. I am also a bit disappointed, more poignantly as well, that Goldhaber's treatment of "The Fox and the Crane" carries an extra line. How can all these guests going hungry half the time gain another seven percent body mass? [One-fourteenth is approximately seven percent and the poem carries one too many lines to qualify as a sonnet.]

Use of syntax, the arrangement of sentence elements, and use of diction, the choice of which words to use, are two of the most common performance standards for the modern poet. How does Goldhaber treat syntax and diction? For the most part very naturally; however, there are instances in which each seems strained either by the demands of the form or to enslave, or enslaved serve, the rhyme. This *is* the exception overall to her mastery of the form; Judith Goldhaber is beyond a doubt triumphant over the sonnet. Unfortunately, that very skillfulness tends to call greater attention to those verses within the collection that fall short of her ability.

Examples of some of the diction I consider strained are somewhat, admittedly, picking at nits. Most of the examples have to do with using French words that are less common in regional usage—in the Midwest at least. In "The Wolf in Sheep's Clothing," page 20, she uses "*ragout*" as a synonym for stew to rhyme with "who." I would be more comfortable with burgoo, but—*c'est la vie*. Another frenchism is the use of "lavaliere" in "Belling the Cat," page 4, to rhyme with volunteer. Somehow, I can see the cat using the word, but mice seem a bit rustic for calling a belled collar a lavaliere. Were there more justification within the poem itself, this would escape notice; however, it seems as arbitrary as the end rhyme and forced into it for the sake of a rhyme with *volunteer*. What if she rhymed "tinkling lei" with "Friday" (re: Robinson Crusoe). My least favorite diction faux pas is the jolting use of "sybarite" in page 126's "The Ant and the Grasshopper." [Consider that this represents three syllables in a work of well over 14,000—one three-beat cord in an opera as it were.]

Strained syntax is a rarity in this collection, but it is there to find. In page sixteen's "Androcles and the Lion," the first line strains with "Fleeing from his master's *bondage cruel*," which is obtrusively archaic in sound. Add to this the twelfth line's "to pieces he'd be torn" and the sonnet's closing "leaving the slave eschewed," and the entire sonnet becomes a wart on the Galatea which is *Sonnets from Aesop*. The word "eschewed" itself is strained in its usage and is likely too 'cute' as one of my college professors put it, but one truly must appreciate the pun intended.

It is rather rare in today's poetry world to find poets with a gift for, or honed skill of, rhyme. What a delight it is to find a collection of 100 poems with actual rhyme schemes! Poems that recall Donne rather than Seuss! Somewhere in the neighborhood of 70-75 percent of the poems use the rhyme scheme earlier discussed: A-B-B-A-A-B-B-A—C-D-D-C-E-E. Every poem here begins with the same octave, but what follows the octave varies in several. The following sonnet is exemplary for the form, as well as somehow apropos of current international politics:

THE DOG IN THE MANGER

The yellow straw that filled the Oxen's manger
looked like a comfy pillow to a Dog.
She stretched out for a snooze, happy to hog
the bed. The Oxen, sensing there'd be danger
when she awoke, and hoping they might change her
attitude (since they were all agog
with fear and hunger) tried a dialogue,
offering to share their dinner with the stranger.
The Dog, though, being wakened from her sleep,
became enraged, and chased the helpless cattle
out of the barn—a most unseemly battle
since dogs would rather dine on pigs or sheep
than straw! But dogs, like men, will oft destroy
the pleasures they themselves cannot enjoy.

Page 28

More important than the rhyme scheme is the author's grace of execution in those rhymes. Considering that there are over 500 rhymes in this hundred-poem codicil, it becomes quite clear that the few strained rhymes are quite insignificant to the work as a whole. What I find most fascinating is the use of rhymes that are neither perfect nor imperfect enough to classify, in my mind, as rhyme versus slant rhyme or sprung rhyme or near rhyme, etc. I advocate calling them slip-rhymes. The best example is, page 96, the rhyming of "affairs" with "prayers." Also notable: *beast / leashed* (98), *voyeur / that fur* (98), *elementary / gentry* (170). This is even more fascinating given the fact that regional pronunciation makes such a difference in how distinct the slight difference in sounds.

Further proof of the poet's skill at rhyme exhibits itself in the wonderful mix of feminine (double-syllable rhyme) and masculine rhymes throughout. She uses feminine rhyme exceptionally well and judiciously, especially in her octaves. One might take her to task on stretching things too far in her few exceptions of stretching the rhymes such as in "The Rabbit and the Frog," with *galvanic* rhyming *volcanic*; it might work better if they were not concurrent line ends. But Goldhaber otherwise executes in Olympic excellence. Take for instance:

> "I would," the Fox cried, as he started running
> "but sometimes I'm outfoxed by my own cunning."
>   —"The Fox, the Cock and the Dog" (2)

> of heather, grass, and other veg<u>etation</u>
> around her forest home, a timid Hare
> was spotted by a Hound. At once the pair
> took up the chase. Propelled by desp<u>eration</u>,
> her legs the only ticket to salv<u>ation</u>,
>   —"The Hare and the Hound" (92)

> Thus did a Serpent, frustrated and f<u>urious</u>,
> unleash his fury on an iron File.
> But wise Athena told him, "Save your bile;
> nothing you say or do can be inj<u>urious</u>
>   —"The Serpent and the File" (104)

[Note: I opine that the finishing couplet could be better polished as it strikes my ear with more dissonance than any file rubs my skin.]

It truly is a sign of great talent that any poet could carry such consistently tight and well-rhythmed verse through a project as momentous as *Sonnets from Aesop*. Note also in the above examples the poet's aptitude with enjambment. True proficiency! Judith Goldhaber uses her colors well in painting verse. She knows very well how to shade and highlight, when to blend and when contrast, whether to brush or dab her hues; she demonstrates masterfully throughout the collection the various skills she has learned. What's more, there's a spirit of fun here that begs one to believe the poet was crafting with as much love as skill. The few exceptions to excellence in singular poems seems to me a sign of fatigue or distraction and never, having read now at least 110 of her sonnets, would I believe any to be a case of lapsed skill.

Would I be a scoundrel if I were to ignore the illustrations by Gerson Goldhaber? Of course! It was the illustrations that carried the book over the finish line at the 2006 Independent Publisher awards as a the Outstanding Book of the Year for design. Without the illustrations, the poetry holds its own; with them, this is the most marketable poetry publication since shock-dada went out with the Beats! Great work!

Need I mention Aesop in all this? He was very well respected by the poet's treatment. The few questionable shortfalls are only worth mentioning by way of fair treatment—reporting the ill with the great. As it stands, *Sonnets from Aesop* is one of the most exciting works I've seen—the Neo Classicist in me is building an *Arc de Triomphe*, figuratively, even now. Bottom line: buy this book. Buy one for your kids. Buy one for your neighbors' kids. Buy one for your nephews and nieces. Buy one for your public library—and the libraries of your local schools.

Petrarch's Sour Grapes

For Judith Goldhaber

Somewhere in Elysium, over wine
of course, poets gather to chat about their craft—
who's penning what, what's finished, what's in draft,
and the usual parlor banter of fine
fellows gathered to gossip, talk and dine.
"Are you keeping up?" "Oh, you must be daft!
I gave it up when rhyme went out and laughed
at their simplistic thought," is Petrarch's line.

Erato dances in: "My sons, have you
considered my servant Judith?" "Why no,"
Aesop laughs, "By Job, we've not. Is it true
she steals my lines?" "In as much as the crow
steals its feast!" she sings. "Where your blossoms grew,
she plucks well." Petrarch growls, "To hell she can go!"

Note: Upon reading Judith Goldhaber's *Sonnets from Aesop* and contrasting her rhyme scheme to Clement Wood's rather rigid definition of a sonnet. Petrarch is portrayed as a formalist, Aesop as a Romantic of sorts. Erato is of course the muse of sonneteers for the most part, though some may credit Terpsichore—which is far too risky as the syllable count for her name alone contraindicates its use in the sonnet or any verse form rigidly pentametric.

Marilyn Blowing the Shofar

"*Like blowing razzberries* is how you shape your lips
and teeth and tongue to make the shofar wail,"
she'd read somewhere, so, eager not to fail,
she frowns with concentration as she grips
the horn so tightly that her fingertips
turn white—a resolute female
declaring with one long-drawn-out exhale
her firm intent to throw away the scripts
written for ladies of a certain age.
The shofar's cry of joy and pain and rage
rings through the temple, while her shining face,
pink with exertion, redolent of grace,
suggests we might transcend the spoken word
and simply howl in order to be heard.

Judith Goldhaber

THE HANGING OF MARY SURRATT

They all wait in hooded darkness.
But the day must have been bright.
Dark chivalry for the lady,
for Mary is shielded by a parasol;
the others are directly under the July sun.
Colors must have been vivid,
but this photo is black and white.
Eyes are primed for the trapdoors to drop.
Lincoln is always about to be avenged but never is.
This photo only promises death.
It's the next photo that fulfills the promise.
Witnesses, soldiers, the magistrate who gave the final nod,
are dead, dead now longer than they ever lived.
There is strict equality under natural law,
living is a first-degree felony
Mother Nature a hanging judge.

Richard Fein

PISTACHIO CRAVINGS

Pistachio shells humped over in darker dirt.

he's gone

He's gone, and pistachios stone the ground light-brown.

no sound

His teeth struggled to open lips;
He sucked away the salt;
His tongue, his saliva, his jaws,
the same utensils used to take me.

but he's gone

long gone and full I'm sure along the way

in the way pistachios relieve only pistachio cravings

Pistachios litter the soil
Like cigarette butts canvas curbs;
Used metal and plastic
Half buried in earth or concrete scrap.

waiting

To smear my eyes with smiling;
To fuel my brain with scenario;
Needs fulfilled: butts will rot,
The other crap crumble.

He's never been gone long

Anita Stienstra

DRAWN IN LIGHT

Paintings of window light
fill the floor
more and more matters
of life.

Bucolic barometers
of my beating brain
trying to unburden the spirit
of life.

Of life
we spend three fourths
in seeing than a'thinking
and less in thinking than a'seeing
drawn in the light.

Anita Stienstra

LIFE IMITATES LIFE

The phone fits her ear
like the other side
of a seashell
her brain inside oyster soft
in thought — or were they words —

which came first
she wonders too much
sometimes forming ideas
for so long they pearlize
and she wears the emerging strand

as a crown around her intellect
striving to be both
mermaid and jellyfish like. The sea
itself pulls her through the current
she longs to enter and exit —

this two-way conversation
she thinks of as deity-delivered
enough to snivel when you disconnect
with oceans filling her eyes
wrinkles becoming gills. Perhaps

the rising waves of e-mail
will speak to her body
smooth her into sand
join her to the inorganic —
she speaks its language too.

Anita Stienstra

I Fell Beside an Ocean

In a dream of life, stardust-born and hurtling
through space, I penetrated the blue ovum—
Earth's atmosphere, and slid down the sky slant
a million miles an hour. Hitting sands
beside an ocean, screaming with the pain,
loss of freedom in the birth of temporal
existence. The noise of screams, cries of pain,
new sensation . . . first breath, lungs air-filling.
Wonder died in that moment. Life became
emptiness and separation, longing
for fulfillment and the struggle to breathe.
But then God offered Her breast, I drank deep
of milk, love, and compassion. Life went on,
beginning when I fell beside an Ocean.

David M. Pitchford

Love And Longing On The Loop

Bud Bartlett

My reunion with Stacy Kross happened over doughnuts. I was eating breakfast in one of those coffee shops in Chicago's Loop where the restrooms hide from everyone but the health inspectors. It was a sort of tan vinyl oasis in the concrete canyon, an odd place to find someone who had come up from St. Louis to photograph yachts.

She poured my coffee wordlessly—the wise waitress' tribute to customers who have brought their heartaches and hangovers downtown for another day, and who stave off defeat for a dollar a cup. I watched her bob and weave down the aisle.

Waitress-watching is a furtive pleasure because it is always done in public places. Sometimes those white institutional smocks cap a bottle of acid; sometimes they emphasize bounce. Something in this particular bounce made me try to guess her age.

Thirty-five or so, I thought—a little younger than me. A single man in town on business could do a lot worse. Was this wishful thinking, or was there something familiar here?

By the time the cup of coffee was gone, I had decided that I knew her.

That wasn't really such a far-fetched idea. I grew up in Chicago. With the exception of two spinster aunts patiently guarding a brick apartment block, all of my family was long gone. But if no longer of the city, I was in it often enough.

By the time she brought the breakfast, I had sifted through some of the memories, trying to recall the time it must have been. I didn't remember her from the four married years I'd had here. Margaret and I had never really blended our life styles. To me, her people had been mostly ski bums and other jocks. She thought of my newspaper and filmmaking friends as cafe drunks. There wasn't a single friendship begun during our marriage that had endured beyond the divorce. This tantalizing recollection came from before that. College, probably.

"Hey, uh, you got any cake doughnuts left?"

She turned in mid-stride. "Plain or frosted?"

"It doesn't matter."

She went to the counter, where there were some seats

empty, and spoke to the other waitress. "Sue, we got any doughnuts left? Cake doughnuts?"

Sue probed vigorously among trays of muffins and other pastries in a display cabinet, and was rewarded. "Plain or frosted?"

"Either one."

"Well, we got one of each, Stacy."

"Put 'em on a plate, will you, Suse? Thanks." Borne on their last journey by two hands and one plate, the doughnuts floated across the room.

Stacy! I made the connection just as she reached my table. She was Stacy Kross, Eddie Pritchett's girl friend. She put the plate down, nodded at my "thanks" and stayed to add the charge to my ticket.

"Aren't you Stacy Kross?"

She looked at me. There was no recognition in her eyes, which were green—another fragment of memory. I presented my credentials. "Didn't you live on Ashland and go to Loyola?"

She lowered her pencil and order pad all the way down to her sides. After a long, long moment, she smiled. "You lived next door to Eddie and gave us that radio when his fell off the window sill and broke. You're . . ."

"I'm Harry Slivak, Stacy. The last time I saw you and Eddie must have been sometime around '81." Her hands stayed at her sides, and her back was still turned to the room, so I pushed on. "I thought we knew each other, but I wasn't sure."

"A couple of us have told Mabel—she's the hostess—that we ought to wear name tags," she said. "Do you ever hear from Eddie?"

"He called me once, maybe a year after graduation. I couldn't see him because my wife and I were packing for a weekend trip. He said you were still together, but he was thinking of going into the service."

"He did that," Stacy said. "He went into the Navy. He didn't have much luck outside of school. We wrote for a while, but they started getting shorter and shorter. There wasn't a lot to say, after a year or so." Her smile disappeared, as the memories tugged at it. "That really was a long time ago. Do you and your wife have any children?"

"No wife or children," I replied. "We were divorced. That was a while back, too."

She must have seen something in my face that I didn't realize was there. She stepped back, and pulled my order from the pad. Then, she spoke from what is properly described as a good heart. "Well, there are a lot of single people around. I'm not sure why, but I never married at all."

One of those memory fragments fell between us. I had seen her sometimes in the vestibule of the apartment building, in the morning, while she was waiting for Eddie. She would have been waiting to prod him along the way to class, and being downstairs was better than being upstairs, because my apartment was next door to his. I knew she had been with him all night, and she knew that I knew, but pretending otherwise was her way. As I left, there was usually the almost physical compulsion to look at her from the waist down, perfectly packaged in jeans. Recalling that took just long enough to nearly lose me the opening.

"I'm just in town on business, and the business ends at sundown. Will you have dinner with me, Stacy?"

"Oh, I'd love to, ordinarily, Harry," she said, "but my boyfriend is coming back to town today. That makes it special for both of us." She smiled again, but not at me.

"Lonnie and I have been going together for so long that I have to remind myself of exactly when it started. He's a groovy guitarist, and he travels a lot. He sings, too. He's been on tour for almost two months, and he's coming back this afternoon."

I couldn't quite let them go, the memories and the moment, so I said, "Well, maybe some other time."

She said "sure," but her gaze—and her little smile—were focused somewhere beyond me. I knew that under the circumstances I was making a forlorn gesture, but I pressed a business card on her. I'm a free-lance writer and photographer, so the address and phone number on it were for my home. I said so.

"But the name here is 'Harry Simon'," she mused, looking at the card but, maybe, seeing something else.

"It's a professional name, Stacy. There isn't much need for them in my line of work anymore, but I got it established quite a while ago, so I just let it stand."

"Yes, I know. Lonnie calls himself 'The Outlaw' when he sings."

We said our good-byes and our hope-to-see-you-again-soons. I left a much bigger tip than was necessary. Then, in pursuit of my magazine article on fresh water yachting, I went off to the Lake Michigan shore and made a lot of polite conversation with people who used words like *ketch* and *slip*.

If you're both a magazine writer and a photographer, you wind up doing a lot of features on pretty places. Pretty place stories serve a useful purpose, of course, but a steady diet of them fattens without satisfying. To me, they have the same relationship to solid photojournalism as soap opera does to Broadway.

I unloaded the color film from my camera that afternoon feeling that I had met a deadline without accomplishing much. It was all exposures of pretty places.

In the absence of anything specific to fill up the evening except for a standing invitation from Aunts Sally and Martha, I decided to put some time into a project which was, in a way, my own Broadway play. I loaded black-and-white stock into my camera and took a cab to Union Station.

I had been working on a photo essay. I was calling it "The Faces Of Travel." Mirrored in my negatives and prints would be people facing transition. The hope for escape would be there, and the fear of the unknown.

Everybody thinks of Chicago as a railroad city, and it still is, but the reality doesn't quite square with the image. It is mainly a city of freight railroading now. Most of the great passenger trains are gone, and some of the great terminals that served them. The 12th Street Station with its clock tower was knocked down years ago, the Dearborn Street Station is some kind of mall, and the Northwestern Station serves commuters exclusively. For long-haul trains to other cities, only Union Station survives. Its great hall, with the polished wooden benches and granite columns reaching up three stories past a gallery, looks something like it must have in the heydays of the 20th Century Limited and the California Zephyr.

I took a series of long shots from the gallery and then wandered down among the benches. Finally, with my shoulder bag clasped shut and my camera hung around my neck, I went down the wide ramp that leads to the platform entrances and ticket counters. Ahead of me, through a gap in the throng, I saw something interesting. Three people came in from the platforms and stepped on the escalator one at a time, so that I had a look at each of them. The man was dressed like a fashion magazine's idea of Joe College Student, in tailored jeans and a plaid shirt under a leather vest. The women were a contrast, with one in a tasteful deep green suit and the other looking like a macaw. Her electric pink pantsuit was topped by a red sleeveless jacket. She teetered along on color-coordinated platform shoes. Her hair, piled high, was approximately the color of a new aluminum saucepan. The other two were carrying the luggage.

When I got a good look at the woman in the green suit, I took my hands off the camera. It was Stacy.

I had an impulse to follow them that was compelling, irresistible. I stepped on the escalator, too.

In the era of the great trains, passengers and their families went into Union Station by the broad stone steps that descend from the street level doors to the great hall. Now, most people take several flights of escalators to or from a glass booth in a little plaza next door to the old main station building. That route runs past underground shops and restaurants. The rush hour was subsiding, now, but there were lots of people coming and going. I lost the threesome.

I stood to one side of the stream of people, feeling fairly stupid. This impulse was something like my childish maneuvers to see how well she filled out her jeans, years ago. The comings and goings of this threesome were none of my business. I hitched up my camera bag, and somebody touched my elbow.

"Harry?"

Stacy stood there. "Lon and I were just having a drink, inside." She waved at a sort of watering-hole-cum-hot-dog-stand, the kind that edge concourses in all passenger terminals. "I saw you walk up."

"Well," I pulled the camera from around my neck, glad it was still hanging there, and tried to push it into the shoulder bag, where it refused to go. "Your boyfriend—Lon—came in on the train?" I finally got the damn camera put away, and she ignored the dumb question. "Why don't you sit with us? Have a beer on me?"

"Well, thanks, but I don't know, Stacy. I was shooting for my . . ."

"Please, Harry." The tone of her voice—and the way she avoided my eyes—made me nod. She led the way inside.

The bird with the bright plumage and the boyfriend were at a corner table. By chance or design, I got the seat opposite him.

"Harry Simon, this is Lon Duggan." Stacy didn't introduce the woman.

Duggan extended his hand between his drink and the ashtray. This place didn't care much about anti-smoking ordinances. Up close, he looked like fifty was going to be his next milestone. I shook his hand as he was presenting the other woman. "Harry, meet a new friend of mine. This is LuAnne."

"Nice ta see ya, Harry," she said. "You a newspaper reporter?" She pointed at my camera bag.

"We got a lot in common, LuAnne and me," Duggan said, looking at her. "We both sing. We do the same kind of music."

"Do we evah." LuAnne giggled.

"And," Duggan continued with a musician's timing, "we came in from Joplin together." He abruptly left off studying her galvanized hair and looked at Stacy. "But like I told you Stace, it's real good to get back to the big town. Hey, order us another round. On me." He glanced in my direction.

"Thanks," I said.

"Hon," LuAnne pouted, "you cut me off. I asked, uh, Harry if he's a reporter." A definite silence fell down around the table.

"Not quite," I said, poking a small hole in it. "I write for magazines. Sometimes I take pictures to go with what I write." It was the standard explanation for people that I considered nosy, or just didn't like. Pictures took the place of photographs, and I left out the word article, which, to those who cared, would have set me apart from the O'Henrys and the Hemingways.

"That must be groovy work," Duggan said, not meaning it.

If nothing else, being a writer who must draw information and opinions from real people gives you a sense of the range of personalities who are out there. Duggan didn't hide much of himself, it seemed, and he was a type that I thought I had seen—and heard—before. Belatedly, he sensed the possibilities.

"Hey!" he added, "You could write about me and my music."

"And on mine," LuAnne said.

The round of beers arrived. "Maybe I could," I said, looking at my glass. Although Duggan had made the offer, I didn't see him reach for his wallet. Stacy must have paid for them.

Duggan lit up a cigarette. "I'm really a lot of color when I sing, man. I do the classic sound. I derive a lot from Baez and Guthrie." He treated us to a smile which had the geometry and warmth of a picket fence.

In a second I sensed LuAnne would chime in, so I presented another standard reply. "We could talk about that. I work out of St. Louis, so unless you were down there it would take around two-fifty in advance for travel and expenses." No truly professional freelancer who is on to a good story idea would ever ask the subject to pay for it, but I doubted that Duggan would know that. He didn't.

"Two-hundred, fifty?" he asked.

"Yes." I was damned if I would consider writing about him for four times that. In advance.

"Well, maybe we can talk about it when I get some gigs lined up in St. Louis." He stuck his cigarette back into his smile, ruining what was left of it.

I took a pull from my beer, and contemplated the half-glass or so that was left. I wanted out of this pathetic situation. Of course, I wanted out of it with Stacy. All of this had come from wanting a cake doughnut, it seemed. Why had it turned out to be so much, so damned difficult? Duggan was ahead of me. The man had a plan, and said so.

"Now, like I said before, Stace, I promised to make sure LuAnne gets home safe with her guitar, and all." He motioned at the duffel bags and instrument cases on the floor beside the table. He took Stacy's hand, obscenely. "You want to go with us, or go straight home and wait up for me?"

They're living together, I thought. Here is a good-bye for the Prince Charming-in-waiting, me.

"It's gonna be dark," she said. "I can go home if Harry will walk me to the subway."

I was, I thought without joy, going to be useful after all. Perversely, this may have been the reason I had wished a lot, way back, that Eddie's girl was my girl. She was fresh. She knew what to do. The contrast had been there, at the apartment building entrance. Stacy well-scrubbed in the morning after, Stacy whose sigh was heard through the wall the night before.

Duggan and LuAnne stood up and turned to sort out their pieces of luggage. I caught Stacy's eyes. "That would give us time to have dinner, after all."

LuAnne, festooned with a guitar case and what looked like a purple leather valise, straightened up. "Nice meetin' ya, Harry."

Duggan fished up two quarters from somewhere and put them on the table. He shouldered his own guitar and lifted up a canvas bag. "Yeah. Then I'll see yah about ten, Stace."

We watched them step around the tables and out of the place. Stubborn at being ignored, feeling like I ought to look for a pimple on my face, I pressed the dinner idea on Stacy again.

"Did you think that would make him ditch her?" she asked.

"Only partly." Duggan's two quarters stared at me.

She found my hands and held them both. "Ah, Harry, thanks. I didn't mean to play games with you. Really, I didn't."

"Has he always treated you like this?" Wanting to lash out at Duggan, and knowing some of it was intended for her, I tried to take a stand. "This act, this act I just saw, was calculated to make you look like his upstairs maid. Damn it, I'm a stranger. What does he do when people you both know are around?"

"Lonnie didn't ask you to sit with us, Harry. I did."

"Because he brought this molting parrot home with him. All right. This is where I came in."

She turned her face away. I knew why, and, like all men since Adam, I backed off. I sat down again, pulled a napkin out of the dispenser, and pressed it into her hand. "I'm a little sore about being used as bait for this guy, but it's not a bad game. Why not play it to win? Hand him a little crap. Carve up a big filet with me somewhere."

For the first time since she had found me in the concourse, she smiled. It expanded and became a grin. "I'll bet you've forgotten what a filet costs in downtown Chicago. You'd pay a lot of dollars to hear me talk about somebody you don't like." With the neat suit jacket and the beige blouse collar, her make-up smudges were like decorations put up for a party that had been cancelled. "You remind me of Eddie, and I really loved him a lot."

"They're my dollars," I replied, "and you haven't said no."

"I have to say no, Harry. Maybe you could understand it if I could find exactly the right way to explain it." She looked at the tabletop. "There's no reason why you should pay to help me think. But you could walk me to the subway."

I remembered her saying, in the coffee shop that morning, that they had been together a long time. I thought about my empty hotel room, and I said I would take her to the subway.

Chicago's Loop is really an elevated train line that circles the older downtown. To me, because the El platforms are dwarfed by buildings, the "Loop" has always been a sort of forest, made up of obelisks and columns and cubes. We put our arms around each other as we walked through it, presenting to those still on the sidewalks a picture that said love but wasn't. Maybe that was her private signal to talk.

"I guess that I'm a couple of years younger than you. Give or take. You wouldn't remember that I didn't finish at Loyola. Eddie was ahead of me, too, but he just about didn't get his degree. When he didn't do anything with it, when we didn't stay together, graduating didn't matter to me anymore."

As we waited for a light, she looked up at me. "I didn't understand this then, and I haven't tried to explain it to anybody else for a long time, but I really got scared of being alone. Taking the lead, the initiative, didn't do anything for me. I finally understood that Eddie didn't want it, either. I realized he wasn't going to come back from the Navy. He found somewhere with people and security, but I wasn't part of it. I tried to fill up his place with classes, with people I knew. Pretty soon I knew that the pushing and filling weren't going to give me any guarantees. All of the people I cared about seemed to go off somewhere like Eddie. To the damned service. To Miami. To marriage. I held on to guys too hard. Thirty got closer. Then Lonnie showed up. He made me furious, once or twice, when he pulled this stuff. But I found out that he's like me. He won't stay away. He doesn't want initiative any more."

I recalled how quickly he had dropped the idea that I could write something about him. Most show business folk are persistent about publicity. Fame is a goad.

"He'll be at my place later tonight, and maybe we'll patch it up until the next time. It isn't so much that we'll be there together as knowing that he will show up. We live there. He just plays somewhere else."

We crossed State Street and came up to the vestibule that covered the subway entrance. For a moment, I knew panic at the idea of leaving her there. The next time I was in Chicago, maybe she would be gone from the coffee shop where I met her. Maybe there were a hundred S. Krosses in the metropolitan telephone directory.

"Thanks, Harry. Good-bye." She kissed me.

"There are lots of trains. We could still have dinner," I whispered, holding on to her.

"Maybe we will, Harry," she whispered back. "I have your card. I won't lose it, and I won't forget."

Her eyes touched me for a second, and then she hurried down the stairs. A train was pulling through below. I waved, mute.

Then I stood by the curb, noble and romantic and rejected. The truth—soured with self pity—was that I had wanted to talk at least some about me. We hadn't done that, and now we wouldn't. I was alone, but she was going to be with someone and alone at the same time. It was a rotten pair of alternatives.

So I didn't want to walk anymore. I hailed a taxi for my hotel, and checked out of it. I picked up my car and pointed it at St. Louis. When I finally allowed myself to think, on the interstate, I thought about the profanity of our needs.

Somewhere, later, I did have dinner, but it wasn't steak. It was a couple of sandwiches I bought from a vending machine.

Ten Ways to Knock the Block

David M. Pitchford

What is Writers Block? Seems a simple question, doesn't it? But it is not. We all seem to have an idea of what WB is, but how do we define it? The condition of being blocked from writing? This raises the question of what causes such a block. The answer to this is both simple and complex: the same thing that causes any mental block. Sometimes WB is as simple as the indiscriminate loss for a word—a condition easily remedied by use of a dictionary and/or thesaurus. Tougher forms of WB can stem from numerous sources, anything from sleep deprivation and fits of micro-sleep to burnout or amotivation.

How do we deal with WB? There are as many formulas for this as there are writers. Likely more. Breaking the block is mostly a matter of self-knowledge. By understanding ourselves, we can learn what causes these blocks. Knowing is half the battle, as the saying goes. If we study ourselves as we write, we gain a great deal of insight into our personal writing process—and thereby learn what starts, stalls, and stops the process. We can then take that knowledge and apply a reasonable problem-solving strategy to knock the block and get to writing.

Below are ten basic strategies to deal with some of the most common causes I know for WB. Most have to do with caring for the physical self as a catalyst for maintaining the mental self, whence all writing flows. And that is the goal of knocking the block: maintaining flow. Keep the machine clean. Keep the software clean. Keep the power on and uninhibited. These are the outcomes we desire and which facilitate healthy, productive writing sessions and careers.

These are, of course, merely suggestions. Use them sensibly and responsibly if you choose. Though I recommend keeping yourself healthy, any advice I give on nutrition or exercise comes with the caveat that you are responsible for your own health. As such, you might want to consult your primary physician before heeding such advice.

You know yourself. If you don't know yourself, start learning! Experiment with yourself. You are the most willing subject you will ever have for the experiments it will take to get you to "having it down to a science." Enjoy yourself. Enjoy your own writing. Learn to take great joy in both your successes and your object lessons (they are never failures if you learn from them).

1. Run Away
2. Write
3. Read
4. Stop
5. Suck it up!
6. Re-organize
7. Breathe!
8. Listen
9. Eat
10. Bathe

1. **Run Away**: Exercise stimulates the mind as well as the body. Stimulating circulation by exercise naturally stimulates the brain by increasing bloodflow to it. A bloody brain is a healthy brain! So to speak. Walking will suffice for beating the block. The point is to get away from the pen or keyboard and initiate physical activity. I, and many of the writers I discuss these topics with, find that physical activity also relaxes the mind in a way that facilitates the natural filtering of thought from the thought-blocked unconscious to the re-focusing conscious mind. It's somewhat like opening the pores to your brain by increasing the bloodflow and decreasing the direct tension by flexing muscles elsewhere. This is, of course, common sense. But we all need reminded of life's "lower" functions now and again.

If you suffer from a particularly stubborn block, I suggest finding new scenery in which to walk, jog, run or work out. I like parks any time the weather is not overly atrocious. In dire circumstances, I can walk or jog in rain or snow if the wind is not howling. The change of scenery stimulates my mind while the physical exercise gives my metabolism a lift, which in turn increases focus and keeps me alert. Possibly because I am Cancerian, a park with water, either stream or pond, works best for me.

Physical exercise is also particularly effective when writer's block stems from a sudden change in direction. Often I have to break sessions into specifically writing, and specifically editing sessions. Exercising works like a charm to enable the transition from creative to mechanic mode. It is much healthier than the old habit I gave up a year ago: smoking a cigarette. Take care of your body, take care of your mind. Take care of your mind, it takes care of you.

2. **Write**: Writing little things can lead to bigger thoughts. Sometimes just creating a list is enough to get started. This is much like walking a few blocks to build up to running. It's not exactly the goal, but it is necessary to keep from straining yourself on the way to the bigtime. Try writing mundane, inane, or gibberish things just to get your fingers 'in touch with' the keyboard. Again, this is like a stretching exercise, but it can be pragmatic as well. I often begin with a list of activities I plan for the day. If this overwhelms me or fails to generate ideas, I move on to wish lists and lists of household chores I want my house-elf to execute (my house-elf seems to be nothing more than myself in automaton mode between mental exercises).

These lists often become story and poem ideas—occasionally even poems unto themselves. They also act as a compass for me if I lose track of what it is I want to accomplish any given day or week. Keep in mind that, like any to-do list, these should remain flexible. Be reasonable if the list is to be functional, but permit yourself occasionally to create extravagant wish lists, which are healthy for Imagineering. Often writing lists opens your subconscious mind by requiring it to answer questions in regard to goals and priorities. It's a sort of psychological slight-of-hand that I find wonderfully useful.

3. **Read outside the Box**: It is all too easy to get sucked in too close to the material about which we are trying to write. We just can't see when we're too close to it. So back off! Go read this week's New Yorker cartoons. Or your

horoscope on MSN.com or anything that is not your subject at hand. Read an article on travel, cuisine, or relationships—just make certain your reading is a hard shift from what you're attempting to write on. The shift in thought patterns will help you shift your focus in such a way that you can go back and focus more effectively on what you're doing.

Holding too tight can cause you to lose your grip, so lighten up. I think it was Frances Mayes in *The Discovery of Poetry*, or perhaps *that author* in *Sin and Syntax* who uses the term "composting" in reference to letting ideas settle. You don't need to be an expert in the psychology of the unconscious to understand that sometimes we overfocus on a topic or subject to the point that we lose sight of it. How many of us wake up at four in the morning with that elusive word we wanted to use yesterday? Or the perfect solution to a character's dilemma that actually fits the character's character? Or the perfect answer to a plot twist that we were working on last week? We all have those moments; it's the subconscious working, in its inimical logic and objectivity, to solve problems, questions, and curiosities unresolved in our waking hours. It's truly a wonderful and miraculous process, and one of the most powerful tools we have. Learn to use it—if you listen to it, it will tell you how.

I strongly recommend, ironically enough, against studying books on writing. Notice I write studying. Browse them. Peruse them. Read one idea at a time and let it percolate. Incorporate one strategy at a time. This is the whole secret to self-improvement: deal with one powerful change at a time and build upon it until you assimilate this improvement into your being. Pick your greatest weakness, or the one you find most intolerable, and attack it with single-minded rabidity until you've turned it into a strength. Then move on to the next.

---

*This technique is one I use when writing: as I could not readily recall the author's name, I use a place filler and asterisks to denote the need to update. I have since researched the book to find the author's name—*Sin and Syntax: How to Craft Wickedly Effective Prose* by Constance Hale: ISBN .978-0767903097

4. **Stop**! Prune the roses. Guilt and responsibility are tough taskmasters. Sometimes it is simply impossible to write past them. It sucks, but that's a fact. Deal with it. What is it that keeps you from writing? Does your lawn need mowed? Roses need pruned? Tree or shrubbery trimmed or hacked? Driveway need swept? If your subconscious is trying to tell you something, listen! It's your closest, best ally. Trust it; it is you. Trust yourself. If the roses are calling, answer. If you've put off checking the tar job you did to patch the roof and it's a good day to get up there, take care of it and then come back to your writing. Congratulate yourself for being responsible and then dig into the writing—maybe even by writing a narrative of the episode.

Sometimes stopping for a brief respite is the only way to continue on any given journey. If your 'urgent' list has caught up to become your 'important' list, then stop and take care of business. Occasionally our subconscious struggles with the goals with which we program it and sends us signs that it is too conflicted to go on the present path—this is one source of writer's block that is very difficult to overcome at the keypad, daisywheel, or journal. If the thing your subconscious is telling you to do is simply not reasonable due to conditions, try writing your subconscious a note with specific times and conditions under which you will take care of the task. In essence, write yourself a contract.

Last year I kept getting blocked because my roof is in less-than-prime condition. I could not sit through a sunny day and continue to write without that little voice in the back of my head grousing at me to get up on the roof and spread some tar. This went on for several weeks. My goal was to write 2000 words a day on my novel, which would get me to a 100K wordcount within two months. I began to think my goal was completely unreasonable. I fretted and worried and stagnated. Then one fine morning I said something like "forget this!" and stomped outside. Half an hour later I cleaned the tar off my hands (no mean feat) and sat down to my laptop. I made my goal, and then some. By the time my wife returned from work I had made up six days of being blocked. I finished the final 30K words of my draft within a week!

5. **Suck it up**! This is the lousy weather answer to number four above. Carpet need cleaned? Clean it. Need to sweep the floor? Sweep it. External clutter often symbolizes internal clutter; if we clear the external, then, by metonymy, we clear the internal clutter. It's a simple sort of magic, really. "Cleanliness is close to Godliness" and all that—clear your clutter and invite your inner godliness to come and create your writing with you. Vacuum the house. Put your stacks of books (those not immediately relevant) back in their proper shelves.

There are always about a hundred household tasks we can knock out. Sometimes racing through these mindless tasks settles our minds to the point of opening that wonderful fount of infinity we call imagination. Wash the dishes. Do the laundry. Clean the toilet. Sweep the floor. Dust the bookshelves. Rearrange the cabinets (this is especially fun if you have a spouse who comes home to find everything where it doesn't belong). What else can you do? Clean the litter box? Brush out your dog or cat—sometimes this will settle their spirit enough so that their pouting doesn't play on your subconscious.

If you're afraid you'll get too side-tracked by household chores, you can always clean up your desktop. How many of us could better organize our files? Build more manageable folders? Delete or archive old files that seem to push themselves into deadends? Run a scandisk on your computer to keep it running as smoothly as possible. Keep the flow...

6. **Re-organize your workspace**: Cut the clutter! Karen Kingston has a couple of great books that deal with this subject: *Creating Sacred Space with Feng Shui* and *Clear Your Clutter with Feng Shui*. The latter is one of my favorite books because of the ironic humor in having it in our house to begin with. No other book seems so ubiquitous; it seems that any time I undertake the task of re-organizing piles and stacks in our dining room, which serves as my second and third offices, *Clear Your Clutter with Feng Shui* finds its way to the bottom of the pile. I'm not really into Feng Shui, but my wife is hip to it. I humor her, because I love her. Mine are the

books on runes and tarot cards and a dozen or more biblical sources, philosophy, poetry, etc.

But I do believe in the power of the mind, the power of metaphor on the mind, and the power of suggestion, as well as the universal flow of energy. Many of the writers to whom I've spoken have offered explanations as to the way such things work. I certainly believe that if you believe something works for you, it works for you. It is likely to continue working for you until your belief is eroded by experiences you believe to be contrary to such beliefs. Try it out, see if you believe, if it works for you. Pay attention to how your own energy flows, and how it flows in relation to the things around you. Despite what our cosmic froufrou sources on numerology say, I work better facing south than east (although, in all honesty, the books suggest that this might have to do with the disparity between my current name and the name I was given at birth).

Keep in mind that you are who you are. If you organize your space, organize it for yourself, and not for anyone else. Organize in a way that facilitates your (better) habits. In extreme cases, it may help to organize the way you think your spouse, roommate, mother, neighbor, etc., would want you to, but this is a stratagem best used for cases of hard blocking caused by taking the same path so often you've worn yourself into a rut. In which case you need to jump out of the rut and go a different way to refresh your perspective. But in milder cases of block, you merely need to organize according to your own system. Beware your lazy self and its lies about having no system. If you had no system, you would be very challenged ever to find anything. What looks like total mayhem to everyone else likely has at its root a very simple or very complex system of associations for you. Changing the system is likely to be a time consuming strategy of procrastination as well as most likely being ineffective for any length of time. You have a natural flow and system. Figure it out and work with it.

7. **Breathe**! You'll be amazed how much a good, deep breath can invigorate you. It seems that in these days of super-technological advances our bodies as well as our minds

are often refreshed by the basest simplicities of our animal nature—especially given our tendency toward tortured posture at the keyboard.

Take ten deep breaths. Count as you inhale, hold for the same count, then exhale for the same count. Hold for the same count and then repeat. Many of the New Age materials use ten as a good measure; depending on your lung capacity or speed of counting, you may want to try five, seven, or fifteen. The point is to fully expand your lungs and improve your oxygen saturation, which helps with circulation, which helps optimize brain function, and so on.

If you're into that, a little chant or psalm sometimes helps. Play around with it. Make it your own—and then write an article on it . . . Having asthma, I tend to be rather inconsistent with this; however, it is one of the most effective strategies for the space of time it takes. I can even enact this exercise as I write to keep the flow. The later it gets, the more effective this seems for me. I often stand to do it so that posture permits maximum expansion of my lungs. There's also more than a little research that suggests breathing exercises are excellent for overall health—and overall health is a good thing.

8. **Listen**: What kind of music inspires you? What excites you? Charges your mind? Empties your mind? Knowing these things about yourself will help you to find the right music for the right kind of block. Mental blocks, especially WB, can come from numerous states of mind: over-clutter, void, tangential anxiety (worry over other things), sleep deprivation, sleep surfeit, boredom, amotivation, etc. Find the music that works with the source of your block.

If I'm stressing too much about my bills being overdue, I'm not thinking about writing. How to ditch the anxiety? Nihilistic rock! Anti-commercialism rock—Warren Zevon helps a lot, as does Steppenwolf's "Born to be Wild" (*Ya gotta go make it happen; take the world in a love embrace* . . .). Hard-edged rock also helps sometimes with amotivation; it's hard to be bored with Creed and Pearl Jam thundering behind me. Sometimes my mind bogs down with too many words, to the point they begin to lose meaning. At those times, I either go for offbeat songs with challenging lyrics or music devoid of lyrics such as Jazz, big band, New Age, and Classical. Sleep deprivation calls for anything that isn't soothing (though sleep really is the best remedy for sleep deprivation).

Other times, it may suit you to listen to books on tape. Your local library likely has plenty of these to check out. Find something that interests you and play it as you type. It is incredible how much inspiration you can get from hearing someone's else writing. Whether the subject is anywhere near what you're writing about or not, often the sound of our language seems to help it flow more smoothly as we write. You might even pick up a few words for your vocabulary, or recall some you've ignored too long.

9. **Eat**: How many of us write ourselves into a corner? We start out early in the morning and work until we finally find ourselves staring at the screen or keyboard with vacuous eyes wondering what broke our stride? I do this far too often. What causes it? Hunger. The physical kind. The kind that is my greatest paradox—ally/nemesis. Science has gone a long way to prove what humankind has known since knowing was invented: starve the body, starve the mind. Your body needs nutrition. Protein helps me far more than simple carbs. I've experimented with this extensively over the last four years, and I'm as certain of this as I am of anything: high protein is the writer's friend and sugary snacks are the devil's handiwork. Have the cheese, skip the crackers. Have the nuts, but not the chocolate coating. If you must have carbohydrates, make them the complex kind you get from vegetables! Fruit is good for an energy spike, but if you're going to write for a few hours, I recommend you dip apple slices in peanut butter (the miracle food).

Reward yourself with drinks and sugary snacks only when you have time to kill away from the keyboard. Your prose will reward and thank you for it.

10. **Bathe**: I do not intend in any way to disparage anyone's hygiene. This is about bathing for relaxation. We discussed earlier the adage about godliness and cleanliness;

while that can be applied here, this is more for the benefit of relaxation and reinvigoration. Linger. Enjoy. Use oils or gentle soaps that smell good and make you feel good. Unless you're an ascetic in your writing habits, bodily comfort is your friend. If you're a part-time writer, this is often a fantastic transition between the world of work and the world within. It is a pseudo-ritualistic way to put aside your work persona for your writing persona. Such rituals are indispensable for writers who have day jobs that don't dovetail with their writing—and many of those that do.

MEMORY DRILLS

Partly, you fear the Alzheimer's
that erased your mother's mind
while she still breathed,
so you're memorizing
the countries of Africa,

But also to bear witness
to AIDS, cholera, tuberculosis;
the plague of stealing small boys
from their families, their childhoods,
shoving rifles in their hands
as if toys; the plague of gasping famine
and drought reducing men, women,
and children to skeletons layered
in dusty onionskins of flesh.

So you begin: Algeria, Eritrea,
Ethiopia, the Sudan's Darfur,
Niger, Zambia, Rwanda.
And while you're at it,
you decide to throw in Iraq,
Afghanistan, the Mexican border,
the coasts of Louisiana and Mississippi.

Everywhere, blood and dust
and water rising, drifting,
choking the blood and dust
that we are, the blood and dust
we'll all become:

Africa, our cradle; Africa,
the grave we're digging,
Africa that must be remembered.

Robert Cooperman

CORA MYERS AT THE SATURDAY NIGHT DANCE AT THE LEGION HALL

I figured tonight I'd separate Rick
from his mouse of a wife once and for all,
me with a dress flimsier than what Marilyn
made famous long ago; eyes popped like firecrackers,
peckers applauded when I cat-walked into the Hall.

But Rick had dancing eyes only for Ellen,
leaving me to the stomping boots of a cowboy.
But when Rick's brother Mike cut in on him,
I figured it was time for me to set my trap
outside, so I ditched that shit-stinking cowboy,
and stood like I was waiting for someone else
in just enough light for Rick to see the little
I was wearing in his honor.

In a second, we were groping to my car,
me thinking he'd leave Ellen that night,
and we'd be the happy-ever-after couple
everyone in high school said we were meant to be.

But just when I thought he'd gasp and declare
his undying, if interrupted, love for me,
he was apologizing that he was happily married.
So why was he pawing me, just then?
I slapped him, hoped I'd left claw marks
down his face; explain that to precious Ellen.
Then I found that cowboy, the luckiest
son of a bitch in this county.

I kicked him out before dawn, him hopping
into his boots like a staggering pogo stick.
Then I cried, for wasting my life on Rick,
and sat drinking coffee laced with bourbon,
listening to country songs, and thought,

"Cora, honey, you are one sad cliché."

Robert Cooperman

Mike Gooden Dances with His Sister-in-Law at the Saturday Night Legion Hall

One loving word from Ellen,
I'd take her from Rick,
them mismatched as a mustang
hitched to a full-blooded filly.
I'm clumsy as a two-legged stool
when I cut in on Rick,
Ellen with eyes only
for my little brother.

But even if he did finally
take up with Cora, and I declared
undying love for Ellen
on one Hollywood knee,
she'd kiss my cheek,
call me sweet, and say,
"Any girl'd be lucky to have you."
I don't want any girl, just Ellen.

I see how Rick looks at Cora;
that dope could've had her for life
when they were high school items,
him, our star guard; her, the bounciest
cheerleader ever to turn somersaults.

Had Rick married Cora,
I'd have married some gal,
but when he came back
from that bull-buying trip with Ellen
instead, I was stuck in quicksand
and didn't care if I ever got out;
only I'd never say a word.

Now Rick's sashaying over,
smug as a tomcat. I lumber outside,
grab a beer, but too many chores
at dawn—even on Sunday—
to waste my time at a fool dance.

Robert Cooperman

Like It or Not

There's no air
quite so much like breath itself.

Night cut across her path, blisters on the palms.

She gathers down, lucid,
microscopic
as if to clench tight, she knows,
never holds.

A low-tide levers
sand from under the pressure
of staying what was his body,
now foam and wire-flame.
Recede,
glance and wash.

Why is it always up to her?

Teeter-totter. Sun-spots
warning recall,
a radiance she used to tease
into rhythm, their game.

The glassy sea floats fear-stained buoys —
inside, porpoises suffocate.
Memory beads their breathing.

Change, change, no disaster.

Smooth out, the mantled cloth
dragging everything over the edge.

C. L. Gunther

An Image of Us

I bring nothing.

You receive me in the restless atmosphere
while a bird in the linden tree continues
dreaming. For a moment I comfort myself
with its secret image, a secluded heaven,
while over my shoulder a parched and crackling
angel reads the blueprints of our love.

You are unaccustomed to grievous climax,
crying stirs the silence you prize.
Uncomforted, I paint my lips
as white as the remains of the moon.

Now I have left you and am wrapped
in all the seasonal leaves,
in several dense and calm clouds,
and a bird trembles on the branch awakened
from a foreign film in which someone suffered.

C. L. Gunther

WEDGE

Distance recedes
releasing a downpour
of the heart's pressed gallery.
She folds the blankets,
their heaviness seeming to increase
with every gathering.

No one walks through the door
except the usual handless ghosts.

Exhausted from their moans,
she wedges the pillow
under her neck and imagines
holding the heaviest
of black pearls
tenderly, as she would hold
his head in her lap.
But even this icon
is beyond poetry's reach.

C. L. Gunther

Sitting by a Lake in Las Vegas, New Mexico

The pale sky arches cold with light
cloud sweeps.
Two scissortails swoop
and bounce the air currents
to alight
on a piñon tree struggling in sand.

I lean back and feel the roots scratch
and reach water.
I feel in the sand
the rippling water
the shadows of children and sand.
Flat rocks whirl and skip at the skin
popping circles in circles
that radiate out
before struggling their weight
to sinking collapse
at the bottom of the lake.

John Dean

MOLLY SINGS FOR THE WARD

She sweet plucks the strings
she's felt
heartache, sings she now for air,
for better breath, her heart cries at
the past, her old sojourner days —
    Molly lulls the souls of hurting
        folk who seek the balm, the
            song-tales soften pain
        like amethysts, each story
    brings them hope as
               her guitar strums
          wondrous tunes that speak
         from far the long ago
        to heal like magic.

Hugh Jones

Go By Art's

Sloped house to tease
 one's mind, Art has
 crusted to a sorrow,
 smoky windows frame
 a man with coarsely
 peppered uncut hair.

Art types short words that
  pop like cinders
  from his big old
Underwood, oh they be
    spit-spun stories,
    one-time reads in
    soggy pulps that
    crassly trace Art's
    schizoid life, once
    meanly lived.

Some murmur there's a
  lady who has stayed
  with Art for years. Oh,
  she sometimes comes
  downtown alone and
  will stop to chat a bit,
  if you'll first look at
  her and smile

Hugh Jones

Death Wish

"Lo, I am abhorred
more than the stench of crocodiles,
more than the foulness of an adulterous woman."

  Four thousand years ago
  peace reigned in Egypt.
  Crops abounded,
  cattle multiplied,
  the arts flourished.

"My friends believe the slanders against me.
My wife will not look at me.
My sons are ashamed to bear my name."

  Elaborate festivals
  wooed countless gods for protection.
  Sadness offended them.

"At the festival of Horus
bowmen atop the temple walls
whistled arrows past my ears.
I wept in terror.
My enemies say there were no bowmen;
they say my tears were blasphemous.
Alas, I would rather be guilty
than unjustly accused."

  The gods appeared as rams, falcons,
  goggle-eyed dwarfs, giant serpents,
  crocodiles, hawk-headed mummies,
  lionesses, female vultures,
  and crowned animal-headed people.

"Hordes of gods pursue me across the fields
howling, hurling obscenities.
A cobra tightens round my skull."

  Just as the Nile recedes

and its waters return,
so man appears to die
and is reborn.

"Sweet Death,
as a man longs for home
after years in captivity,
I long for you.
Envelop me
like the perfume of lotus flowers,
like a soft breeze in mid-summer.
Enfold me as a mother her newborn babe.
Sweet Death,
come—"

May R. Kinsolving

The Garrulous Man

Once there was a garrulous man
who talked before the cock's crowing began
and talked through his breakfast of oatmeal and tea
and talked through his dinner of beans and barley.
He talked all day and he talked all night
and this garrulous man he had a wife,
until one day she conceived a plan
to escape the talking of her husband.

She stood a mirror behind his plate
and in the evening as he ate
and talked to his image in the glass
she opened the door and fled. Alas!
The talking man kept talking on.
He never knew his wife had gone.
Since his image kept listening, as images will,
he talked and he talked and he's talking still.

May R. Kinsolving

ONO NO KOMACHI

As Japan's most revered poet,
she wrote only of love
and the pangs of passion denied.

When her litter passed,
men made obeisances so elaborate
they seemed dance.
All extolled
her flawless features, swan-like neck,
slender waist, dainty instep.
Scores brought gifts:
mother-of-pearl combs and hairpins,
carved pipes in embroidered cases,
fans decorated with cranes
and misty landscapes.
The most persistent she sent
on vain errands to distant outposts,
reviled them on their return.
Many waited night and day
in cold and snow outside barred doors;
an elderly suitor died of exposure.

As her skin wrinkled
and tales of her cruelty spread,
would-be lovers deserted her.
Then she wrote of the desolation of age
and the fickle hearts of men.

Very old,
she wandered in rags, unrecognized,
begging for food,
mocked,
stoned by children.

Now,
her bones dust,
her only remains
faint lines on crumbling paper.

May R. Kinsolving

The Female Horseshoe Crab

Caught, bled, and thrown back
this survivor rises
at spring's high tides,
breaks glistening
from the sea,
shell shield tough,
males in tow,
to lay her eggs
in fine-ground sand.

She swims away
but returns and returns,
well provisioned,
eggs enough for attendant
willets, sanderlings, and gulls,
who poke at once
into rich nests,
feasting on the plenty
from which these crabs
will go on, as they have
for eons,
the young ready
to begin their molting,
mounting year by year
til they're ready
to answer the spring tides
in armored squadrons,
ready to be bled,
to feed the shore birds,
to go on.

Graham Duncan

Note: Drug companies bleed these crabs for the clotting and antibacterial uses of their blue blood. The great majority of the crabs survive the bleeding to go on to lay their eggs and to be bled again in following years.

Going On

> *"Keep death before one's eyes daily."*
> *— Trappist rule*

Another night arrives
misting our naked eyes,
but our instruments
see through that haze
and even stellar hazes,
searching out beginnings.
There, words are being spoken
in a language we cannot parse:
the black holes sunk
in the larger blackness
all we'll ever be given—
even as words we cannot speak
well up from our private blackness
to move our throats and lips
as if articulation were ready
to slip, starlike,
into its rightful place.

Then night fades as light returns,
and forgetfulness fools us—again
we set about our purposes
played out in this wisp of light,
cajoled by its blandishments,
something like meaning on our lips
as we grope for auspicious words
and squint at spectral hints,
trusting our eyes.

Graham Duncan

THE BARD'S WORDS

We have them. Or do we?
No manuscript survives.
No writings, new born, dewy,
beam up at us. What gives
us thrills and chills arrives
by means of others—a scribe's,
actor's, printer's guesses,
teamwork of a sort, piled
up, barnacled, filed
down again, great masses
of collaboration.

A mighty force, a nation
of scribblers making messes?

Scholars, linguists, critics—
all compelled to witness—
seldom say so, having
glossed, repaired, and raved
about immortal verses,
our sweet talk and *his* laced
tight, manacled in place,
never to be unbound—
in cadenced sense and sound,
rich lingo richly sewn.
We've made his work our own.

Graham Duncan

You, Anne Sexton

You, Anne Sexton—
Why are you here? Don't you know
that my passion's run dry?

I take in your craft
like another addiction;
I give you—poetess—a run
through my veins. Yet it's
all too often my image I see,
my thoughts by your hand, heart
nailed to your words.

Why, Anne Sexton—
on page 153—are you
wearing my mother's image and name?

You're astonishingly,
achingly all too familiar;
the titular mother's got nothing on you.
And when I'm undone
in my mind's dusty corner,

Is that you—Anne Sexton—
teetering posthumously on my windowsill?

Danielle Minzenberger

ROAD HIKE

walking . . .
    sauntering . . .
        on an isolated road

unexpected
    four white-tail does appear
leaping gracefully
    across my path
strong, healthy, carefree
        gliding across a field of soybeans
disappearing into the adjoining woods
    a joy to see

Ken Sibley

FORGOTTEN COUNTRY

Such is the land of fecundity:
Flat to the north, where the glacier
stemmed topsoil yards deep
with untold seeds
of earthly generations

To the south, hilly
with the burrowings of beauty,
horse country trees densing
up and down along
slipstreams swallowing
beneath ridges that chewed.

No one sees this who drives by.
Few who live here know
the bones that belie
under their withering gaze.

Such a monastery of the mind.
A godly paradise of wild
blooming, blowing, feathery
gold prairiemath.

Let us pray to find ourselves here:
Where the sun is long, horizon
drawn with bumps of trees
and strands of cloud
thin as a madam's scarf,

striped barns rounding and mares
nickering and houses that stand alone
eyeing across each field what
we are in this place:

A people plentied by sky and soil,
where growing is a gift
we know without looking,
rivers strain and pull
downward to origins, self a root
among roots en route to our seasons.

David Radavich

CASUALTIES

Leaves spiral
in green agony,

each one
a friend falling

in spring
against everything

I have known
of seasons,

buds banished
in discovery

by the old
who stand barren

as scarecrows,
rooted

too hard and
empty of essence —

this storm is ransacking
youth, tearing out

hair
of the angels

David Radavich

HATE SPEECH

Words have been slaughtered
without mercy.

Crawling on all fours, screaming.

Rose of Sharon—gone.
Emerald butterfly—utterly.

Give me a fair noun
whose hands have not been
chopped off.

Genitals of union
electrified.

Eyes have been ground
into verbs that become jelly.

Prepositions clamber into trees
yelling for safety.

Only imperatives rule
like dictators, like jail-keepers:

Kill others now.

David Radavich

ODYSSEUS WHEN YOUNG

A ship out of Brindisi
rocking in the Adriatic.
Between the islands of pleasure are the worst storms.
Who will dress for dinner?

Twelve on a ship to Piraeus,
Ithaca abandoned, too far off course.
Besides, the dog is dead.
Besides, the old dog is dead.

Spray vaults over the bow.
I am drenched, on the lookout
for a place to grunt and squeal,
a refuge favored by swine.

But I am not yet thirteen.
Who will know us when we arrive?
A man with a lantern who follows me,
who makes his home in a cask.

E. G Burrows

CENTIPEDES

My mother abhorred
    the creepy-crawlies
who lurked in cupboards
    or behind the drapes,
feasting their eyes on her,
    waiting to strike.

She could hear every patter
    of their hundred feet.
They needled her.
    They mocked her fears,
tunneling under the carpet,
    stalking from mouse-holes
in the closets
    where sometimes they slept.

She was the only one
    who heard or saw them,
but she knew they were there
    waiting to sneer and punish
should she falter,
    waiting with a hundred feet
to trample her
    for her failures,
for the sins she was sure she had.

E.G Burrows

CRIME SOLUTION

Someone is kneeling beside the body,
a rose or a knife in her hand.

It's a moor, quite obviously wind-swept.
Grass bends back from the sea's edge.

Her shoulders covered, a gray shawl
blows across her face.

The wind wipes out whatever she says.
It's a death scene by the book.

As detective in charge, I question
every lark, every mute swan flying over.

This is one of those baffling mysteries
so loved by bird-watchers.

Which came first, the knife or the rose?
The body is mine. The knife is yours.

E. G Burrows

MINIATURE

Why
are
all
the
words
for
minutiae
so
BIG?

and
so
many
words
for
BIG
miniature?

Is this an infinitesimal irony,
or merely a fault of language;
wee, though only three
letters, is still too enormous
a word to describe
this little life of ours
little life of hours
seconds inching by —
wee, too powerful in its fun
to describe this life
in miniature.

Fillmore Lewis

How Much

How much
do you want to know

about the cost
of discipleship

in the clothes-basket
where the cats are born?

How much
do you want to know

about your own heart
as it faces

not cold facts, but
warm brooding art?

William Meyer

When Shadows Fall

Sometimes they fall
very short distances

and sometimes they
fail

like a school-kid
who tries to grasp

the sudden hands
of darkness/light.

A cat lies in the grass
asleep, shined-up

—failing to sense
what plays around its claws.

But we see
and think

and feel.
And that's enough.

William Meyer

AP's Person Without

He hears
without
joking

and sees
without
roasting

and fights
without
knowing

and eats
without
glowing

and sits
without
sisters

and sleeps
without
whispers

and gives
without
asking

and dies
without
axing.

William Meyer

A Glass of Heads

Four or five big
white diaphanous altheas
loll in the yellow
drinking glass
in the kitchen window

and my hand shakes
from the cutlery
—the faint red line
around my neck, moistening,
reaching my knees

and Socks the cat tumbrelling

William Meyer

Foul

The looming moon
a puddle behind trees.

I know that flat moon face.
It's desolate.

Wants to ask me all the hard questions.
The answers to which are only black.

Peter Layton

Aspects

I watch the cars,
beads on the highway,
lives

I'm wondering why this was denied me.
Curlicues of thought
from a banged up window.

And all the yesterdays
all you could swallow.
I hear the buzzing of an airplane.

Dust in the air so far away.
It could take me.
I'd be suspended

between the other world and this one.
No actual hugs.
No kisses.

Peter Layton

After

The mountains look blue from here.
Do they know about you?
Do they hear my crying when I can't control myself?

I'm weak.
There are so many left things I have to tell you.
But you've left.

And you've left me knowing that.
And the great sad mountains.
All those years they leaned their last shadows on you.

Now when the tearing winds blow
in their high heights,
do they also cry?

Peter Layton

THE BIG BOYS

after exhausting the shallow woods
the big boys went underground
exploring the sewer tunnels
filled with unspeakable horrors
only the bravest of the brave
would descend into the darkness
and face the unknown
those lacking in years and courage
eagerly awaited topside
for reports from their heroes
who emerged proudly
wearing soiled clothes
like great badges of honor

Jamie L. Mauldin

Business Trip Blues

after dropping you off at the airport
I turn off the radio
to sulk in silence on the drive home
the windshield wipers
keep rhythm with my heartbeat
I stop for Mexican carry-out
to smother my sorrow in salsa

the cats are annoyed
by the disruption of routine
my sullen mood
makes them anxious
they search the bed for your scent
obviously disappointed
by the lack of warmth

the sky has cried my tears since your departure
raindrops pelting the windows exacerbate the silence
without your confident voice
the strum of your guitar,
the sound of your tools
mixed with your satisfied mutterings
coming from the next room

I try to pretend
I am as independent as I was when we met
a complete farce, but not a disappointment
we have meshed into one complete whole
balancing our weaknesses, strengthening our potential
satiating needs unmet for far too long
once empty spaces now filled beyond capacity

days are spent in half-hearted living
nights are restless
without you as my pillow
I count the days, hours, meals
until your return
when joy will descend
like a plague on our home

Jamie L. Mauldin

Things I Have Learned

If it buzzes, it probably stings.
Almost everything can cut you.
Mow your grass long to conserve water,
but if you have ticks, cut it short.
Most underwear is uncomfortable.
Everybody stinks.
Chimpanzees are the only nonhuman primate
you can look directly in the eye
without them feeling challenged.
All babies shit. A lot.
If it tastes really good, it's probably really bad for you.
Everybody dies.
You always run out of ink/gas/money when you need it most.
If it hisses, it's probably pissed off.
It's easier to learn a foreign language
than to become a nicer person.
No matter how much money you have,
it still might not be enough.
Run from an angry dog, and you'll get bitten on the ass.
Lying can be useful.
Every insult is based on truth.
Butterflies metamorphose, you just change.
Cars have a sense of humor.
Lots of pretty things are poisonous.
The ocean doesn't care if you drown.

Karen R. Porter

QUARRELERS

Spitting images of cat and dog,
we sit on the fence all night
hissing and mewing,
barking up all the wrong trees,
until the neighbors shush us
by throwing old shoes and rice,
like they did at our wedding.

Your tears scratch at my eyes.
I growl and gnash the teeth
tearing at my stomach.
Straining at my short leash,
I collar the urge to kill.

They say it's OK to be ourselves.
But what if we act like animals,
mouths unmuzzled going for the throat,
biting the forbidden Adam's apple?

Down on all fours, we crawl
out of our clothes to lick our wounds.
Rubbing haunches, we pat and purr;
hackles still stiff, we circle
sniffing dried blood.

In a minute, our tongues, furry
from liquor, will fly. It will be
tooth and nail again.

Maybe, if we played lion and lamb
we could lie down together a while
and nuzzle instead of always
eating our hearts out.

Arthur Gottlieb

GETTING OVER IT

Once I loved
enough for two.
When you went
I whined the way
a dog does days
after his master dies.

In the beginning
blood beat
a path to my heart.
But after years
a heart learns to roll
over and play dead.

Your kisses
wet and wicked
lifted my spirits.
But with tongue in cheek
the images of lips
I stick with are
stitched scars
on the far side
or your smile.

I became the flame
of your altar ego,
the candle sputter
at both ends of illusion.

The boldfaced type
I once looked for in my
narrowminded mirror
will never be found.

I know now nothing
is no more
than a moment to be
savored later
as regret or relief.

Arthur Gottlieb

THE HIGH GROUND

the mourners had left
i stood alone
before my wifes coffin
i had already sprinkled
some fresh earth on the
coffin,
    given to me by the
Rabbi, and said the Kaddish,
with the mourners repeating;
    later they
will lower the casket into the
open grave; but for now, she still
stands there in the open;
    the sky blue; lonely birds
float around in the sky as
if witnessing the event;
    the lonely markers
of the many dead stand at
symmetrical attention,
looking so neat and symbolically
pretty even in their stance;
    i keep thinking how short
life is; even our sixty years
together seems like just short a
small time in the meaning of
the worlds turn; i cannot believe
in death; i cannot;
    i put out my hand, she
comes to me, holds my hand
and together we walk to the car
and she gets in beside me, and
says with a sigh, lets get away
from here, where do you want to
go, i ask her gently; she waves her
hands airily; oh, anywhere, dear, to the
high ground, far away from death;

i drive away, talk incessantly,
babbling away, i feel her hand on mine,
and suddenly she is gone; no longer
with me; i could swear it had happened,
am i dreaming? i keep driving,
to the high ground, trees, mountains,
feeling her still with me

ed galling

THE ANSWER

once, when my father
and i prayed in the
synagogue

i was ten years old
then,

and not quite at ease with
religion,

i could not understand all
the Hebrew letters,

nor the prayers that were
being said by old bearded
Jews, i said to my father,

why do Jewish people always bow
back and forth with their head as they
pray?

my father looked at me with a
baleful eye, and said,

because, my son, should we fall,
we hope that God will be there to
catch us in his arms.

sixty years have gone by, and now
i can hardly walk, my gait is
laborious, and i use a cane,

his words come back to me,
i can hear him saying it over and over
again,

and i hope it still holds
true.

ed galling

WAITING TO BE WEANED

Hallowed bed sheets, skin crests
to a memory of harmonized, homogenized happiness
between her milky white thighs

Eclipsed lashes painted charcoal or black
folding into sullied shadows
of haunting shapeless things

Relinquished, a clean break,
scalpel to the umbilical,
abandoned and not yet weaned

draped in white flags,
ravaged and raw,

forever reeling
in—

remembering
and returning
to
the regeneration
of nerve
of skin

Shari Koopmann

ANTAEUS

Slowly swallowed by the quicksand of harmony
over years spent laundering someone else's socks
and arguing over lost Tupperware lids

Swallowed whole,
hard and raw

And suddenly and surprisingly you're coughed up like a hairball
an unrecognizable mythical creature—half you and half not
left trembling, undone and unanswered

A painful surfacing, bound and gagged and half-digested
and the metal table uncomfortably cold,
the voice dry and dusty from disuse,
the legs wobbly and threatening to fold

Prick me, you say.
Let me sleep, you say.
I'll count backwards.
But one and none and still conscious
and remembering the warmth as your body was usurped
by the euphoric earth
with her deceptive good looks and oceanic eyes

Expunged and redundant, you are still like the leaves today
as you ask random passersby absurd questions
like those *Highlights* magazines in doctors' offices

Each day—a different stage of decay
as you move even farther from the credits,
the bibliography and index
of photographs and Tupperware lids

But you're still clinging
knuckles white like blisters
until you're caught by surprise
as the earth gives way

and you're falling
again

until all that surfaces are bone fragments and teeth

Shari Koopman

Arborglyphs

She wrote with the point of a ten-penny nail.
It wasn't her father or even her brother who showed her,
but an uncle who'd come back to find, to visit, his trees.
Those who carved with knives cut too deep. Scarring
began to blur, then obscure the marks after a few years.
Basque shepherds left behind an indelible loneliness
in signatures, in caricature, in silhouettes of sex.
By the sixties they'd gone.
Their trees lasted some decades longer.

She traced her name with her finger
to feel the run of her former hand and as she did
thought of the picture of herself in the hall,
her own jet eyes and bangs, puffy sleeves, square skirt,
and the video of their family trip to the Pyrenees,
her mother yanking her by the arm,
like a yoyo, like a pogo stick.

She found the other names,
traced them too, her father, brothers, uncles,
and the old ones who used to sit at her father's bar.
It was a long look at tombstones.
It was like touching something taboo, a tattoo.
Their European cursive, their Basquoise cried out
from soft-skinned aspens whose lolling and creaking
lent their own dour accompaniment.
What wafts in acrid, in musty scents is heftiness of leaves,
context of shadow, the simple complexity of presence
and here beneath her hand and beneath her feet
the smell, the feel of them looking over her shoulder.

Thomas Robert Barnes

A PRIORI

This was one of those moments
you didn't have to tell yourself
you'd be seeing again.
No one agreed to leave,
hours after they said they would.
It just happened and,
it's what they wanted all along.

There's an hour left of sun, of the webbing and wings
of shadow that attach themselves to everything,
the blue glue of afternoon that seems
to slow to a stop while hurrying.

Your hands cock. The rod loads.
I can hear the stiff wind in mine,
lute-like, siren-like, singing.
You fight it, snapping your line
to strip the moisture from your fly
and not tangle in cross buffet,
nor overhanging willow or brush.

There, in the corner, in the sluice of upturned current
is where the big trout sips emerging caddis.
To force the line in but make it wait to match the flow
you pull back and roll the tip to create the coil.

It's wrists and fingertips. It's patience
and timing and will that fit the fly to its bloom
and, it's the other confluence of events waiting
to concur: rising jaw, the infinitesimal pause,
then line gone taut and suddenly electric
with the struggle that moments before
was only implied by last light on water.

Thomas Robert Barnes

TWAINS

Pop was pals with the Scot,
the organist at church
whose wife, the tipsier she got
muddied her tales with bloody this, bloody that
and though weightless as American vernacular
it did make him go red in the neck,
yet not enough to bar, nay refrain him
his regular stops for free refreshment.
His gig gave them lodging over the carriage barn
at Sam Clemens' place. What was
curious to curators, was all banisters and pool tables,
stuff stuffier than grandfathers, except
for the fireplace. It cost Twain plenty to put a window
over the mantle to watch snow flying down
to meet the flame that kept him warm.
I wondered how many times he got
to pay himself a smile to see it work.

The English lady who pressed flowers
lived in a cottage outside Somerset, Bermuda.
She kept turtles in a clawfoot tub in the garden.
Oleander, lemon and banana arched her drive.
Where it met the lane Mark Twain smoked
his pipe and watched school girls dawdle by.
The woman's husband was a navy man.
When he got sick and died she never complained.
We bought lots of pressed flowers.

Like a camera-shy Indian, Lake Tahoe eluded Twain.
His later years make a man understand
the preciousness of what cannot be captured.

Thomas Robert Barnes

Blue October Light

In every exhalation,
every breath of blue,
the azure conjuration
of the wind
is changing hue.

The bluest of the patches,
parlors of the sky,
show bluer by the snatches
of the clouds proceeding by.

The blue in the eyes of notions
in a face of pinkish white
is as blue as the deepest oceans —
Blue
October light.

J. R. Campbell

The Path Gains Its Agent

Travis Delaware

"Ten more days," Quillon Tark whispered.

His guard slapped him hard across the face, splitting his lip yet another time. Quillon smiled through the blood. *See, bright boy, still got all my teeth.*

"Could use another three to five, you ask me," the guard spat in Quillon's face.

"I didn't ask," the prisoner whispered, his voice harsh with long silence and cigarettes.

"You want to leave with all them pretty teeth," the guard pulled out his baton, "you use your tongue to show respect."

"I respect the respectable," Quillon stopped the guard's baton strike with a lightning-strike kick to the wrist.

"That's it . . ." the guard closed the door and moved toward his quarry.

"Think twice," Quillon's eyes glittered obscenely. "What goes around . . ."

The guard pounded him in the face with a quick left jab and arced his baton right-handed. Quillon, face blank of expression, grabbed the right hand and led its momentum into the cell's concrete floor. Bones crunched. The guard tried to yell, but Quillon's fingers were a vice on his windpipe.

"I told you, Skippy," Quillon stood suddenly and smashed the guard into the ground with enough force to crack bone. "I told you: treat me like you want treated. . ."

The guard tried to reach his radio to call help, but the prisoner tossed it out of the cell.

"I figure you got about 93 minutes before you're missed. That gives me time to lesson you. . ."

† † †

Ten days later, Quillon Tark, aka 'Tark the Turk', was released from Joliet prison. No one bothered to notice. No one bade him farewell. No one even taunted him. He was left alone to walk to freedom.

Chicago was the last place Tark thought he'd end up. But Chicago's south side was the only place he knew he had a place to live—and the requisite social securities required by his parole. His late sister's ex-girlfriend had conceded to his requests out of some duty to Brina (short for Sa-brina). He liked the arrangement because it was uncomplicated.

"Train don't leave another hour," a porter told him.

"What's a guy do in a train station with no money for an hour?" Tark wondered aloud.

"Dressed like that?" the porter pointed at the trademark release clothes Joliet had adopted the previous year to demark recent parolees. "Hustle b . . ."

Tark slapped him.

"Damn it," Tark put a hand on the porter's shoulder, "sorry, bro. Tight nerves. Long time with unsav'ry comp'ny. . ."

"Ain't no thing," the porter grinned a broken-toothed smile. "Guess I know your colors now."

"Right," Tark looked around the station. "All these folks going to the city?"

"Hell no!" the porter cackled. "Most on they way elsewhere. Mostly these suits goin' to the city."

"Thanks," Tark handed the man a small, carved figurine.

"What?" the porter cocked his head in confusion.

"Raven," Tark said, shrugging. "Not the best, but what can you do with pine chunks and half a fork? Only thing of value I had for a tip."

The porter stared for a moment as the parolee walked away. Though he noted the strangeness of the man's bearing in such clothes, the porter was more intrigued by the man's full set of teeth and social etiquette. Used to the rudeness of city folk, the apologetic ignorance of tourists, and the curt insincerity of suburbanites, Karl Smith Jones IV was rarely surprised by the mysterious ways of human nature. He shook his head and moved on to take care of business.

†   †   †

"Excuse me," Tark smiled at a smartly dressed, middle-aged man. "What brand of cigarettes do you smoke?"

"What?!" The man looked up crossly from his Morolla Raspberry, checked Tark's attire and turned in his seat as though facing away from him would solve the problem.

"I asked . . ." Tark said, his voice more gravelly now.

"Yeah, yeah," the suit said. "What kind of cigarettes do I smoke. I don't smoke, Con, so beat it."

"Ex-con," Tark leaned inches from the man's face and inhaled deeply through his nostrils. "As in *parolee*. You smoke Djarilis from one side of your mouth—Standards from the other. . ."

"How?!" The man stood up and moved to leave, but Tark put a light hand on his elbow and looked him in the eye as though in warning.

"What do you want?"

"Let's have a seat outside and smoke a Standard together," Tark said blithely.

"A what? I don't . . ." the man pulled away, but then looked around and thought better of it. "Fine. Let's do that."

"Thought you might," said Tark. "You reek of secrets, my friend."

"So—what, you want to be my confessor?" the suit remained aggressively defiant.

"Relax," Tark said, taking in the long first drag of his acquired Standard. "I was in for larceny . . ."

"Doesn't mean . . ."

"Right," Tark blew smoke in the suit's face. "I killed twelve cons inside and that's why they outed me. Three more and I'm a triple ace."

"Oh," the suit took several quick, nervous puffs off his cigarette before calming himself and trying to frame his situation in business terms.

Tark looked around the station, smiling at the little things he'd missed from the inside. A dove broke through a mob of pigeons to land on the arm of the bench beside him. He clicked and cooed as the suit finished his cigarette.

"What do you want?" The suit said evenly, his nerves renewed by the cigarette and the intervening time. Something about the dove landing so close to the strange parolee made him more comfortable, but it also was strange enough that he felt spooked.

"I need an agent," Tark smiled.

"An agent?"

"Yeah," Tark held out a firm, yet soft hand. "Quillon Tark, karma eater and healer of the damned."

"Right," the suit shifted on the bench, looking over his shoulder for help. "I really have to . . ."

"Relax, Jimmy," Tark put his hand lightly on the other's shoulder. "I read people pretty good. You're the one honest—well, relatively, anyway—suit in that little hornet's nest. I want you to be my agent."

"Agent?" Jimmy's face lost composure as soon as the other spoke his name. Fear and indecision vied for dominance as he tried to use his words to make sense of the situation. "Agent for what? I'm a broker for Hutch, et al. What can I do for a larcenist?"

"You ever see me steal anything?" Tark laughed.

"Well, no . . ." Jimmy sputtered.

"Then I'm as innocent as you, Jimmy."

"You're starting to freak me out a little, Mr. Tark," Jimmy complained.

"Sorry," Tark shrugged. "Been in bad comp'ny too long. Forgot how to interact. Never was on the A-list for *plays well with others. . .*"

"What kind of agent do you need," Jimmy asked. "I know a few guys in a lot of places . . ."

"I need," Tark moved within inches of Jimmy's face, his spearmint breath strong and hot on Jimmy's forehead and nose.

Jimmy wondered why it didn't smell of cigarettes. "I need . . . a priest, a yogi, and a franchise lawyer."

"I think I heard this one last year," Jimmy stood abruptly, but Tark pulled him back onto the bench.

A sudden ruckus interrupted their conversation as a dozen or more men burst through the station doors and argued vehemently on the platform. Jimmy pulled his cell phone out to call 9-1-1, but Tark took the phone and stuck it back in Jimmy's pocket, telling him to let it play out.

A large man with a Russian accent yelled over the crowd for silence. Two small, olive-skinned gentlemen in Yitranah suits drew curved knives from inside their coats. A tall rabbi, traditionally dressed, clapped his hands over his ears and began reciting scripture. A young blond man in a weathered Amarini held his arms out to show empty palms and attempted to negotiate with everyone else. A short, eastern gentleman in a cheap department store suit smiled softly and watched as the others went on with their conflict.

"This compromise," the Russian gentleman said in his thick accent. "This compromise is far from permissible to me and my constituents! You will either forfeit the scroll or die standing here."

"Now Ivan," the young blond man said soothingly. "Ivan, you don't . . ."

"Dmitri, dickhead," the Russian pulled a pistol from his jacket and shot the blond man in the face before turning to the rest.

Tark looked on, smiling wildly as the Russian fired until his clip was empty. The rabbi and the short easterner were struck with bullets, as well as a smartly dressed lawyer, but the others escaped intact. Tark stood up and moved toward the carnage as the Russian snapped a second clip into his Kobranski 11-mm pistol.

"Best pick up those casings," Tark said casually, kneeling down to inspect the seeping wounds of the easterner.

Dmitri looked down the Kobranski barrel at him before laughing and doing as Tark had suggested. He then holstered his large pistol and departed.

"What. . ." Jimmy stuttered, his face pale and hands shaking.

"Power mongers," Tark shrugged, moving from the easterner to the rabbi. "World's full of them."

Tark knelt to the rabbi, frowning deeply. He bent to sniff the man's breath, then moved to the blonde lawyer. He stuck his finger in the bullet hole, then pulled the man up to look at the back of his skull. There was no exit wound.

"Surprising, isn't it?" he said to Jimmy, who had just returned from getting sick on the side of the tracks.

"What's that?"

"Hole like this in a guy's head," Tark pulled his finger from the entry wound. "And he's still breathing."

Jimmy gagged but swallowed hard against his stomach's upheaval and knelt to offer assistance.

"Western medicine—no chance," Tark sniffed the blood from the lawyer's wound. "He's got less than nine minutes . . ."

"But," Jimmy broke out in a cold sweat. "But I don't even hear sirens yet."

"Exactly," Tark nodded. "So either you agree to be my agent, or this poor bum finds out what's behind door number *death*."

"What can you do?" Jimmy's face turned red, his eyes hard. "You can't pin the blame on me; that Russian guy shot him."

"Sin of omission, Jimmy," Tark smiled. "Hurry and decide. That rabbi has less than a minute more than this one."

Jimmy looked at the rabbi, bleeding visibly now from beneath the black attire. He shifted to focus on the short easterner, who was sitting now in an open-lotus position as though under a peaceful rain of blossom petals. Jimmy noted the bloodstains on his cheep suit, the white tie stained crimson.

"What in . . ."

"Decide, Jimmy," Tark whispered. His voice reminded Jimmy somehow of a story about a serpent in a garden somewhere. He wanted to run away, but he knew he was responsible to do what he could to save these men—no matter who they might be.

"Okay," he licked his lips and swallowed hard against the knot in his throat. "Okay, I'll deal with you. My terms are: first that you call me James and not Jimmy; second that I act as your agent on the condition that these men live beyond their wounds—and third that I am indemnified against . . ."

"Spoken like a negotiator," Tark laughed. He stuck his finger in the lawyer's bullet hole again. This time the hole grew closed until it pushed the finger free. Tark grasped the man's head between his palms and closed his eyes for a moment.

He rolled acrobatically over to the rabbi and pressed his left hand over the man's liver, pulling him to place his right hand on the exit wound. He relaxed and breathed deeply, then pressed on both sides and closed his eyes to concentrate. His sense of urgency seemed to wane when it came to the easterner, but Tark stooped to him also and murmured a strange, musical chant into his meditative face: *no fields of rest this moment, my friend*. When he stood up, all three of the gentlemen were whole.

"Well, James," Tark smiled tiredly and fell to the ground, blood running freely from his nose for no apparent reason.

† † †

"James . . ." Sirens brought him from the pooling darkness. No time to luxuriate.

"Mr. Tark . . ." Jimmy placed a hand on the other's shoulder.

"Out!" Tark barked, straining to rise. "You have to get us out of here."

"Me?" James Daniel Branski was never a risk taker.

"Yes," Tark grabbed Jimmy's arm and pulled him down hard; Jimmy braced himself and straightened to keep from falling. Suddenly they stood facing each other.

"Grab the rabbi," Tark pointed. "I'll haul the other two. Take them to that lot—" he pointed with his chin—"there's a midnight-colored Mercandi . . ."

He shouldered the greater bulk of the lawyer, then grabbed the easterner's wrist and dragged him like a recalcitrant dog on a leash. Somehow the slighter man, though of normal height and weight, seemed to float, featherlike, as Tark pulled him along.

"What are you waiting for?" Tark stared hard at Jimmy, who was standing beside the Mercandi panting and watching the other three catch up.

"I don't have keys . . ." Jimmy's tone was somewhere between petulance and accusation.

"He does," Tark pointed his chin at the supine figure at Jimmy's feet.

Jimmy fetched the keys and pressed a button twice to unlock all the Mercandi's doors. He shoved/stuffed the rabbi in the back and jumped into the driver's seat, adrenaline enough coursing through his veins to make his every motion decisive and fluid. Some part of his mother residing in the most noisome part of his soul stood with hands on hips, lips pursed, offering advice as well as exasperation at the once-clumsy boy now speeding away from a crime scene . . .

"Jimmy!"

"James!" Jimmy barked the correction like a dog used to impotent threats. "My goddam name is James: *j-a-m-e-s!*"

"Yeah," Tark smirked. "But you really want to be Jimmy, don't you?"

"What . . ."

"Come on, J-man," Tark ruffled his hair in the way a big brother would. "You're sick of staying clean around all these dirty bastards. You wanna be a gangster. You wanna be Jimmy and let all those liars know that their precious James "JD" Branski was a Jimmy all along."

"*Who* are you?" Jimmy almost stopped the car, but it had been too long since he'd been in control of anything. It felt too good to stop. Moving was his control now.

"Just a guy like you," Tark smiled and let his chin fall to his chest, relaxing into the unconsciousness he'd held at bay.

"Where to now, fellas?"

"Lola's over on Michigan Avenue."

Jimmy jumped, his recoil causing the car to lurch. Quickly, with reflexes born from years of metropolitan driving, Jimmy righted the car before glaring into the rearview to stare at the strange easterner. His pulse normalized as his eyes locked on the reflection of the others' and he smiled.

"Lola's?"

"That is her name—yes?"

"I haven't seen Lola . . ." his mind drifted into a decade-old memory. Lola was his one adventure, a sort of gypsy/hippy girl who ran a summer headshop down on the lakefront. She was esoteric to the bookends, with nothing but karma/dharma protean-kundalini and gods-knew-what metaphysics using her for some sort of nexus . . .

"I never really believed in all that shit . . ." The shiver running up his spine admonished him as poignantly as the eyes from the back seat reflecting into his through the rearview. "Really," he looked the easterner in the eyes, "I believed that she believed, but I could never quite . . ."

"Wrap your *mind* around it," the easterner nodded sagely. "Truths of the spirit find little faith in the mind."

Suddenly the Rabbi sat bolt upright and launched into some Hebraic prayer, which awoke the lawyer with a start. The three looked at each other, turning and nodding and seeming to share some deep knowledge in their wordless noddings. Jimmy looked back to the highway in time to cut off a Jaguar SJX on the way to his exit. The car filled with a strange mix of interfaith singing as he drove the final distance to Lola's place. Jimmy was amazed he could find it; he'd never known Lola to have a regular address . . .

"Jimmy!" Lola shrieked, throwing her arms around his neck and pulling his lips down to hers. "I've missed you so much!"

"Sure you did," Jimmy blushed. "You got some scotch? I'm not having my best day . . ."

"You want some for your friends, too?"

"Oh," Jimmy looked over his shoulder to find his four strange comrades sauntering up toward the apartment. "Well," he scratched his head, "I guess dead guys might care for libations now and then."

"You kook!" Lola slapped his shoulder playfully, then kissed his cheek with more intimacy than anyone had ever touched him.

"Lola," he stepped to the side to introduce the others, but Tark took over for him.

"Tark," he nodded. "We've spoken numerous times—I appreciate the visits in solitary."

"You called me," Lola blushed, snaking her arm into the crook of Jimmy's elbow as though announcing her affiliation with him alone. "I just did what any polite medium would do . . ."

"Your innocence is the only protection you have from the predators I know," Tark shook his head and shivered. He moved toward the door, "Will you have us as your guests?"

"My house is open to all who are free of malice," she smiled and made a sweeping gesture of welcome. "You, too, Jimmy," she winked at him.

"There's someone I'd like you to meet . . . Io! Daddy's home!" Lola laughed as Jimmy looked perplexedly into the apartment suite. Ten years ago, they'd taken in a pregnant bitch and planned to name one of the pups 'Io' and adopt it—but then Lola had run off on what she called *a deep investigation into the psychic war of the Age.* Jimmy still clung to the opinion that Lola had run off with Glow Sorrensen simply because he was scary good with runestones.

"Daddy!" Jimmy braced himself just in time to hold onto the blond fury that flew from nowhere into his arms and began kissing his face all over. He held for a moment before holding out the girl at arm's length—and stared into his own eyes reflecting back from the fey face of a girl perhaps a bit over nine years old.

"Someone . . ." Jimmy's eyes brimmed with the day's emotions. He grasped the glass Lola handed him and drank deeply of the smooth, strong liquor. Recognition of the taste of Glenfidich seemed to encourage the tears to run freely.

"I," Tark put an intimate hand on Jimmy's shoulder. "I am the Path to Home, Jimmy."

"So what is it you need from me?" Jimmy felt full to the brink of total void. His newfound sense of fullness somehow drove home how empty his whole life had seemed to now. He would have sobbed, but lithe arms wrapped around his waist in the one familiar embrace from his life, and all he could feel was something he could only call *homecoming*.

"We are gathered here . . ." Tark raised his glass.

"We gather now to cornerstone a fortress of Truth and set to right a million little wrongs . . ."

Jimmy filled himself with Tark's words as the man spoke for what seemed hours. Each time he looked around, Jimmy saw more faces crowded into the suite on Michigan Avenue. By the time Tark had finished and everyone had hugged and congratulated and exonerated everyone else in the gathering, Jimmy had made his way to the computer and accessed the proper database.

"Here begins the *Path to Home*," Jimmy said, handing forms around for each to sign.

"Looks like I have my agent," Tark smiled.

"You can call me Jimmy."

Fiddling with My Life

An angel stands in the corner, playing
music—I can't tell, is it violin?
fiddle? The tune changes each time I do
a different task. Perhaps it is searching
for my own song somewhere between its wings
and the world around me. Standing still
for one or two seconds I imagine
complete quiet—a stillness in which no
sound penetrates my psyche, where even
she cannot be heard above the silence.

Tucked into this corner, she keeps playing
moves back—forth, sorting me out in-between
the soulful violin and the jazzy
fiddling with my life—keeping me here.

Siobhan

Mascara Stains

Mascara stained pillow case, dampened
with this evening's rage
inner turmoil spilled out
across our marriage bed — the other side
of slammed-shut doors

Irrational actions lead to hiccupped sobs
guilt — blame
anger — shame
an unpleasant mixture
wants and needs
unfulfilled
words we cannot swallow
choke our dreams before we fall asleep

Crumpled tissue piles
soggy on the nightstand
remain to be an early morning reminder
what passed between us
hard evidence
of the shadow-words imprinted
on our memories

Siobhan

I Picture Crows

Stark against the winter sky, branches sway
a stiff breeze blows up to rattle last leaves,
those faithful few, clinging to emptiness,
shift in the fading light of shortened days.

Shadows play tricks on the movement within
their outstretched arms. Unbalanced images
flutter past my field of vision, hiding
truth in darkness, capturing my mind's eye.

I picture crows, each row of autumn leaves
rustled up against one another, not
yet cold—anticipating the weather
ready, even if hesitant, to go

Then—as the last piece of sunlight dips down
to the edge of the world, they, too, take flight.

Siobhan

Affair of the Dark

I came at you—an open womb wanting
just to taste the sweet take of your breath, an
inspiration of something other than
the stale, cold wind of self-exile—not

because you were anyone I thought I
could love, the lover I most desire I have,
but because you I thought might admire
in some Platonic fashion soon to turn

Greek of a moonlit night under secretive
stars somewhere south of heaven where the only
sin is resisting temptation—the flesh
surely longs for the beauty of language

as much as the mind lusts for sex
and its convocation of consummation,
that writhing pleasure dome of flesh
in fluids mingled of life and worship

but your words held me at bay and baying
to the maddest moon, a stray dog scenting
his bitch for heat and howling with the insane
cause of endless generations—and yet

again my words—my words brought you
sniffing, huffing, longing
to share some piece of me
I might let you have despite
an elsewhere commitment, which meant
everything as nothing to us

both—honor the lower priority
to the ache of need—but still some honor
here where honor betrayed
there—it all depends upon which
pocket your hand is in—
so the midnight missives through every time

of day and our desperate calling in the non-
telegraphic silence of subconscious . . .

Oh! this all to sublimate one more day
one more night and rise again on Sunday
but I am not that god
neither pure nor evil
but beneficent in my own
manner and blessing with carnal anointment—come
let me anoint you and introduce you to
mysteries as my muse *du jour*

and I will have you my consort
even as you me in the semblance
you ask, each promise no future
nor past but sweet memory when memory made
and the wry melancholy future nostalgia
when we look back then to realize how close

we were

to the garden as we gazed on
each other's nakedness and you
spoke to the serpent and we
swiftly fled its threshold barely
able to breathe beauty's scent turned
despair, and filled our lungs instead

with the lush carnal mirth of flesh
and bathed in fluid moonlight
under thin sheens of sweat
from our paradisal strut . . . unconsummated yet . . .

Now we in that deep romantic chasm
recall Coleridge Khan's sunny pleasure domes
as you, my Abbysinian maid, play
on your dulcimer loud and long
your symphony and song within

revive deep delight — you win me

and to Xanadu you send me
dancing momently; this mighty fountain
bursts in nature's womb to passions
birth and nurse on full breast
of honeyed milk and paradise.

Years have passed . . . winters frozen
ice creeping its secret ministry
across our hearts — estranged as though
never did we meet, never sin
in our heart of hearts, never lust
and wish death upon the vile
Puritanical prairies that sustain us
one parsed moment from living,
yet fully ensconced in life.

We understand now, you and I,
like a wilderland of broken sky
love stillborn can never live nor die
passion pent is passion perverted,
prevented, turned aside and fouled
like brackish water in an unmoving cistern,
its holiness baptized in darkness
becomes a cancer of the soul
until forgotten —
ours but an affair of the dark
stillborn on unkissing lips,
never to live, never to die,
never recalled but in words —
their absence.

We found no sunny pleasure dome,
yet dwell in caves of ice
yet dwell in caves of ice.

David M Pitchford

Down to the Water, Pray

I saw the sky, saw you soar, saw your eyes
like peacock spots shine green in blue heaven;
harvest of argent mists, stardust falling down
to baptize me for another rebirth—
this one of love and you and truth melded
within a heart open to oblivion
though hoping for a renaissance, yearning
for some sweet tint of violet no eye can see,
one loveliest of roses, an epigone of essences
unnameable, immutable . . . but real
nonetheless! and undiluted as undeluded, please
with a dash of salt and ambrosia to go. . .
I would rather have you for a lifetime
than be timeless, immortal without.

David M Pitchford

Oh My Sisters!

Marcellus Leonard

Your bright black eyes scour heaven and earth
ever vigilant to succor me. My seven Sisters' scolding—
your wings smoldering astride defense. You travel
to secure me from Greenland to Greece. Surely you guard
against even the galaxies, secure the seven seas and coasts,
girded with hope seven times or seventy—smothering grief
on the wing with the love in your wombs—transported
on wheels—whatever the need. Oh my sisters! You are seven
graces—daring love, watchful labor, gratifying birth, strict discipline
arduous training, willful sharing and determined defense.

(Watchful Labor)

My infant probabilities balance on your hips,
within the circle of your arms, and, in lieu of mama's teats,
the bottle in your hand, the warm milk temperature tested.
The bend in your elbow is the river's bend waded—
its depth sounded before you beckon me to "Cross!"
Wherever we travel, you are North before me—always
sojourner first, there to craft cradles, to bounce tears
to vanquish fears and wrestle with the truth—possibilities real
and imagined.

(Gratifying Birth)

      From a narrow fertile, valley poppies race
up a sloped volcano to the summit of its canon
and wave branched placenta before the red outs.
Your eyes silently pursue. Firmly leading me on,
by the grip of your hand, we trudge the wagon rut
determined, sweep the scruff through toward distinct
distant orchards where ripening fruit begs arrival
and gratifying birth.

(STRICT DISCIPLINE)

Black braids twisted like ravens' wings out,
tricycle quick, little sister jumps concrete curbs
to greet me home as I broach the house and that
encourages me. Her feed sack shirt waist mid baby thigh,
vigilant for my return, she eases with a giggle
my day made hard at the steel mills smelting to dross
my sterilized life. In the back of her keen, reflections
of trust and expectations push sparkles despite my bitter day.
Success is not a question. I have to fine the me mettle;
She expects it, demands it in the reach of her soon
becoming — the day dawn side of her determined rising —
raising me with it to noon sky high

(ARDUOUS TRAINING)

You are Noah's raven never returned
preferring endless flight in freedom
to the horrors of that boat. I understand.
I have been drifting too over wide waters
lengthened between continents but find no
Mount Ararat to come to rest on. You are
the rest of my life with wings — the way —
because Noah forced your hand but unwittingly
had trained you first before the dove was sent.
Elijah knows you, the raven in the kitchen
who feeds his children from Her womb
and his from Yours. Becoming skillful, train me
too my sister; teach me how to fly endlessly then
make my opportunity and take it when it .comes

(DETERMINED DEFENSE)

All angels are not men characterized as doves. Some
are female ravens like the one Elijah knew.
In the store parking lot, firm grasp on her grocery cart,
she transforms when a man shoots out his fist
and grab her pocketbook. Right there Eden's angry angel
determines to defend the whole world's larder transported
in that purse, and swords become her hands.

(Willful Sharing)

You refuse to live though gods pursue
so to share in seven sisters' deaths. You hoist
the weight your father hefts and sacrifice yourselves,
for everyone else — you are bright opportunities unmet
but undiminished .

(Daring Love)

"I love you my brother," my sister whispers
still elegant — still eloquent though her dew
skin has long before expended its gifts
and the breathy fragrance of her beauty
has withered on her tongue. My sister Queen —
darling among my sisters before my twilight
and harmonic Ethernet of stars has configured
the older self, how unprepared I am to chase everlasting
without you.

Oh my sister, I never thought you would die first,
your drum thin skin shames Nefertiti's cheekbones —
Teutonic plates carved sculptures in your face.
Where your eyes are, volcanoes spew
then the light ceases and your pupils refuse
to refract light.

DNA never dies and comprises everything there is,
the code for every metabolic megabyte of all existence.
No tears! No gastric insurrection at the lighted tunnels' end
ever brightening. Here give me your hand to boost our connection
like those metallic foil circuits on the back of cell phones.

Making Dust Angels

in the Middle of an Unkempt Floor

Hours? Years? Decades?
He keeps his angels in the unkempt dust
down on Delaware where the old stump
still surrenders booty Bobby collected
playing pirate games at five . . .
At six Bobby bit a bullet
got a bullet in the head, now I'm gone and dead
put a bullet in my head, and now I'm gone and dead
Can't see me cause I'm dead – I put a bullet in my head
in the bathtub — not to leave
a mess for his beaten siblings
to clean up . . .
Knowing less of death
than the condition he knew
as life, Bobby skips silence
across deserted floors
kicks up dust devils to battle his angels,
haunting the place he never lived
but ended life with a .32 Bearcat
Little ghostboy Bobby hasn't a clue
about the nearby college expanding,
land and house assumed as *immanent domain*
and plans for a daycare there where he lingers
Bobby plays with broken glass,
wonders that he never bleeds —
can't reach out to the *breathers*
but that's okay — no one ever listened
when he was one of them, a breather
breath ragged with asthma and reflux
waiting for the next swing of a belt, board, or . . .
a backhoe breaks apart
condemned walls of the only prison
Bobby knows as home.
Who knows why those shapes grace
frosted panes on winter days
in the Delaware Street Daycare . . .

R David Skinner

Bargeman's Castles Made of Sand

With Love to Jimi Hendrix

TC Baylor

took a 45 to my head
bout a hundred year ago
still got that bigbore beauty-
mark on my soul
butterflies and zebras . . .
thought I could touch the sky
but ole iron McClugage
gets in the way

ole man river just carry it away . . .
y'all don' know what goes in there
till you been a deckhand—
till you swep' buckets of coal
till you swep' buckets of salt
till you swep' buckets o grain
off into the river,
into ole man River

coal and grain and salt
dead rats and mice, fish floatin'
topside after another bucket
and another bucket
and another bucket
ah, fuck it—throw it overboard—

"water come and carry me away . . ."

my purple haze got a shit-brown stink
comin' off the Illinois, goin' down to Mississippi
sink in the tombs off dead N'awlins;

my purple haze got a smogbad taste
salt and coal and grain filtered
through a cotton diaper, copper tubing, and
cooked down right in a cracklin' kitchen

fire—fatcat done ate dat rat downtown
an' mercy ain't no word we knows . . .
my purple haze got a shit-brown stink
screamin' *Mary* downwind at the watchtower—
Beauty ain't *in*
Beauty ain't in the eye
Beauty ain't *in* the eye of the beholder—
Beauty *is* the eye
Beauty is the *eye* of the beholder
till it scums with white blind death
and smells of riverbottoms
sewage raw as nature intends . . .

color ain't nothin' but a difference
a difference of this and that
what tells one from other
ain't no color
in the riverbottom
ain't no mercy, no color,
no difference, no justice,
no love nor hate,
sho' as hell ain't no forgiveness

"are you washed in the blood . . ."
ain't no washin' in the riverbottom
go in a king—come out a leper
go in a prophet—come out a corpse
bloated colorless and equal as the day
you was born,
day I was born,
day we all born . . .

all along the riverbottom
currents cry Mary
with its crush of old age and wisdom

will it ever remember
names it has blown . . .

my purple haze has a shit-brown smell
and tastes of carp — scored an' fried up
Peoria knows of rivers . . .
deep as hatred and longer than a slaver's lash
shallow as race-wars
and American genocide,
but with a memory like a catfish —
can live years in dried mud
till the next rainy season

abuse me — cuz I can't kiss the sky!

my purple haze has a shit-brown smell
and tastes of political backwash:
bullshit fed to a starving folk to gain votes
and narry a nutrient in that dinner wagon —
got more bullshit than a rodeo-planet

"shall we gather at the river . . ."
everything gathers at the river
rainwashed till it rolls down
one way or another
"all the shit that floats . . ."
as they say,
as they say
and so castles made of sand . . .
                                          even landlocked in Peoria
fall into the sea
eventually

I met my *Dolly Dagger*
she's a stripper on down the street
and it ain't blood she be drinkin'
from that jagged edge,
no that ain't blood she be drinkin'
she been *smokin'* from a jagged edge . . .

who's got a million days
to daydream, Jimi? Who?

we done seen the scenes
a million kids and papas down
at the whiskey houses
ain't no waterfall,
no waterfall —
and rainbows show
the water bad
                and that's just the good side . . .
hurts as bad
as bad love,
hurts the same
iron pipe or a papa's pride
can get you dead just alike
and your castles in the sand
melt into the sea
eventually

my purple haze got a blood-red stain
soakin' in like Mabel's carpet
soaked her life up
when Little Benny
found a little pink stick
what told him his pimpin' days
was over far as Mabel —
swingin' a hammer jus' easier
than growin' up an bein' a man . . .

another castle in the sand
rots into the sea . . .

my purple haze is a blazin' bruise
where *probable cause* concussioned
me right out of the best job I ever had —

there must be some kinda way outa here
I ain't the juggler,
and I sho as hell
ain't no thief!

man gotta work . . .
but jobs come scarce,
at least

jobs we
ain't fightin'
scavengers for—

"My kingdom is not of this Earth"
I been waitin',
my Savior,
my sweet Lord,
but my flesh is weak
where my spirit is wronged
and the sweet
              everafter
ain't comin' soon enough
to save a starvin' man . . .
who ain't no man
cuz he ain't
got no job . . .
how can a man
be re-spons-ible
when The Man,
who ain't nothin'
but a scarecrow
stuffed with circumstance,
rides us down
his economic
whirlpool?

another castle made of sand
melts into a river
we have known.
river risin',
ice-flow flowin'
wish I was
stone free — do what I please
but some mother's son
sings *Foxy Lady* to my li'l sister
and that ain't right;
at fifteen, Jezel should be in school
not husslin' brothers and others
down dockside, up at Pere Marquette
her pretty little head
should be filled

with butterflies and zebras
fly on, little wing . . .
but when the crack-shot snipers
in a river slum come
to make her a *ho—*

another castle made of sand
sunk into the sea
prematurely

warm clothes and a good bed
don't make a man a man —
what do? What makes a man?
A man?

down here, Jimi,
all the lights are red
and none turn blue
uh — tomorrow
we are the traffic jam
this is the other side of town . . .
all are castles made of sand
flowin' to the sea
eventually —
eventually

under McClugage,
too much clouds your
sea of forgotten teardrops
they ain't no lifeboat
to float home to love
her love, your love
my love, good love
bad love, tough love —
that fern don't grow
where the water's fill
with salt, and coal, and grain
and the bargemen
toss their buckets
and toss their buckets
and tie their lines
and tell you

"it's all good,
Ole man River
gonna come and
wash it all away"
with those castles made of sand
sinkin' to the sea
eventually.

my purple haze got a mud-black stink
and tastes of crow.

my purple haze got a rotten-fish taste
and smells of stolen fortune.

my purple haze, Jimi,
smells of Night Train and
what I got out BK's dumpster.

my purple haze, Jimi,
ain't worth singing
till spring
till summer comes
with barge traffic,
buckets over the side,
jumpin' carp and cussin' boaters.

till then, Jimi,
I'm here
under McClugage,
in my castle made of sand.

Bodhisattva: Eighth Chakra

for Siobhan, in honor of the cover art

I am the eighth chakra — our shared essence
the ether of existence, our mixed selves
the Moment of conscious will. I am All
outshining in your actions and abstinence;
reason in your deepest thought, transcend
with me yourself — you grow stellar with me.
Hear me call in calm hours, stilled-voice silence —
feel me tug your heart to center

when conflict breeds maelstrom
heavy hour becomes manifest hell,
I am your eighth chakra — eternal essence
from which you emerged manifest,
into which you shall egress at that moment
transition so feared — separation, anxiety — Death.
I am you in your eighth chakra — one essence
god watching over your ethereal shoulder

librarian of all experience, of every sense
cataloguer of each datum each moment
ever aware — eternally conscious.
You are me manifest in seven chakras;
travel together every road — pilgrim
seek enlightenment's golden city
spire its rainbowed prism splendor — we too
array our spirit-self as artist bodhisattva.

R. David Skinner

HOME

Joe Kreisberg

I hated every aspect of the car ride. The constant smell of smoke from my aunt and uncle's never-ending cigarettes, a fact only made worse by their insistence that my sole source of oxygen, the windows, be opened just the teeniest of cracks. That is, if at all. There was my backseat companion, my 24 year old cousin Lauren who fluctuated between an overpowering tyrant demanding you listen to what she says and a regressed toddler demanding sympathy and attention. Regardless, she was always demanding and, therefore, always completely draining. The radio never played. Not music anyway. My uncle would allow the occasional Mets game, but between yelling at an overpaid underachiever and screaming at Sunday drivers (of which he himself was one) I always hoped that our drive didn't occur on a game day. Most of the time I just closed my eyes and pretended I wasn't there. It never really worked.

Sooner or later, depending on traffic, we would finally get to the nursing home to visit my grandmother. Some people call them retirement homes but I never really understood that definition. Lots of people retire. Not everyone goes into a place like this. A condo in Florida is a retirement home. An old age home is somewhere you go when your body doesn't work the way it used to. An "assisted living" facility is more accurate. When you walk in through these automatic doors, there is never an old man with loud pants and a hat asking if you want to play a round of golf. Just an orderly asking who you want to see.

Upon arrival, the first thing anyone notices is the smell. A strange brew of filth and sterility. It's a common fact of life that old people smell. I have come to believe that old people are very aware of their odor and try various ways to cover it up. Some old women like to pour on obscene amounts of perfume, enough to turn a hug into a form of grandmotherly chemical warfare. Some older men prefer the smell of cigar smoke or old spice cologne, occasionally a combo. My grandmother was the type of woman who preferred to cloak her scent with a violent bombardment of potpourri baskets scattered throughout her apartment. Any of those scents would be welcome to the one we had to deal with every Sunday.

"We are here to see Sophia Archin" my aunts inform the woman working at the desk.

"She's in her room, you can go right in."

A walk down the corridor to my grandmother's room is always a never-disappointing freak show. Room 235 emits the smell of a man who I am convinced perpetually soils his pants, usually accompanied by what is either his scream or that of his unfortunately broken-minded but even more unfortunately able-nosed roommate. Room 254 always houses a large family sitting around the bed of a comatose woman with tubes coming out of her nose. They watch game shows like The Price is Right in the daytime or Wheel of Fortune in the evening, they talk and laugh among themselves, and children sit on the bed of a women who they will remember less as a grandmother and more as a piece of furniture that happened to be in the room they frequented in their youth. When we get to room 266, we enter and become part of the show.

The bed closest to the door is occupied by my grandmother's roommate Denise. She never has visitors, at least while we are there.

"Who are you! You can't have my baby" screams my grandmother's roommate Denise.

"Mind your business" snaps my aunt.

As we walk back towards the second bed, Lauren invokes her child within and gives Denise the finger.

"Hey Ma" from my aunt.

"Hello Grandma" from my cousin and me.

"Hello Sophia" from my uncle.

Naturally, there is no answer. She lies in her bed and stares out the window. She's gotten worse in the past few months. Before, she used to give us all the wrong answers. Now she talks less and less.

"Ma. It's Ellen. Look Ma, David and the kids came. How ya feeling?"

Grandma/Ma/Sophia grabs her sheet and begins an activity that resembles sewing. In a former life, many years ago, Grandma was a seamstress. It seems that that part of her brain has not yet died. From what I have learned since then, it is extremely common in people who have "lost" parts of their mind. My grandmother cannot remember who I am, but she can remember the motions involved in sewing and hemming, even if she was doing it on a sheet. The woman in Room 134 cannot feed herself but can entertain the other residents by playing the piano in the common area. After the initial amazement, one begins to realize that she can only play one song. Either it's the only one her body can remember, or it's the only one her body wants to play. Another gentleman in Room 103 used to be a lawyer, and every once in a while he'll just start arguing a case to the air. Once again, it's always the same case. From what I can gather, it's something involving a car. Anyone walking through the Nursing home can see more evidence of former professions, often displaying themselves in equally beautiful and insane ways. Hundreds of rooms. Hundreds of stories.

"Let's take your grandmother for a walk" my aunt says.

We take the wheelchair out of the closet and sit up my grandmother. There is no need to dress her because no matter what time of day, she is always dressed in one of her three nightgowns. I wince as I catch a glimpse of a bedsore on her right leg. It's a disgusting reminder from nature that we are not meant to lie around all day. Every once in a while my aunt will pick up my grandmother and bring her out into town to get her hair dyed, her nails painted, or the stray hairs plucked from her chin. "She's lost her mind, but she won't lose her looks" my aunt used to say. I never saw the point.

I often wondered how it was that my grandmother got this way. "An idle mind is the Devil's plaything" repeated in my head as the instant answer. For as long as I can remember, my grandmother never really did much of anything. As far as I could tell, she didn't work very long. All the stories I got of her being a seamstress were just word of mouth from my mother, who seemed to tell the stories as someone who had heard them from someone else. A passed down tale of my grandmother's career. In her 80 years on this planet, she never bothered getting a driver's license. She also never bothered to read books (or magazines or newspapers), do daily crossword puzzles, question the existence of god or even just wonder what the hell she was doing with herself. There was not a single ounce of mental stimulation. There was, however, a sense of survival that I always admired. Grandma/Ma/Sophia had grown up during the depression and, as with many children of that era, it showed. She made sandwiches with the ends of the loaf of bread. She included the butt of the lettuce in her salads. Her fridge was packed with the bare minimum to get by, which usually included some orange sherbet and an Entemann's pound cake (which I suppose in her mind translated to fruit and butter-rich dairy for fiber and the avoidance of osteoporosis.) No car meant walking everywhere she went, developing her into a very fit woman. Looking back, I guess it's easy to see that her body had been trained to stay strong and her mind had been trained to die.

While my aunt, uncle, and cousin would have come anyway, this weekend there was a special event at the home. From time to time, the home runs day-long activities to keep the residents happy (although I'm not sure they even notice) and make the families feel that the money they keep pumping into the place is actually going on to some use. I had been to movie festivals, nonalcoholic speakeasy nights, and picnic days, and they were often more fun than they sound. Unless of course you enjoy sitting around watching the Wizard of Oz with a room full of angry or mindless old people, then I suppose it would have sounded great from the start. Our walk led us to this weekend's event, which just so happened to be disco night. I don't know how this event ever received approval from whatever powers be in the home. I would bet that most of the residents hate disco, the same way my parents hate most of my music. Imagine a party being thrown for you and all you could play was music that you felt was contributing to the decline of the young people in America. If only their minds worked, they would have been furious.

The visitors, such as my aunt and uncle, were having a great time. I guess that is part of the great Old Persons Home PR Machine. If you could keep the families happy, then their source of income would remain intact. Maybe with a few smiles on their faces, they would be less quick to scream "I'm going to sue your ass!" when their crippled mother fell out of a wheelchair because the orderly wasn't looking. Maybe.

The main rec-room was designed to look exactly like a disco. At least from what I can gather from the movies, as I have never actually been inside a disco. A disco ball hanging from the ceiling spread tiny crystals of light onto movie posters of the era. Bad disco music (is there a good?) played on the small stereo system that sat on a folding table, right next to a strangely watery vegetable dip and broken pretzels. A ladle-drawn bowl of punch was also there, which made me instantly think of that scene in Grease where Sonny decides to spike the party punch with a little booze. I think the only thing that was really missing from this party was the braless, sex-crazed girls on roller skates and the lines of coke spelling out "don't worry, it's almost over" for the families to suck up their noses. I suppose it's understandable with the budget cuts. Maybe next year!

The people drink their punch, eat their pretzels, take photographs next to their immobile patriarchs/matriarchs, fantasize about spending a weekend at the beach for once, and all is well in retirement home land. I look over at the radio and something catches my eye. Sitting next to the crappy radio next to the crappy punch is a microphone. The radio I had blown off earlier was in fact a miraculous gift from god. It was a karaoke machine. It was a pretty cheap machine, not even a TV screen showing a random slow-motion abstract scene and the lyrics. Cheap machine or not, I thought it would be fun. A nurse took the microphone and announced that a contest would begin, the winner getting a gift certificate to some restaurant on a strip mall up the block. The party was hesitant to get started but eventually, a tall, youngish looking grandson of a resident sang *Only the Good Die Young* by Billy Joel. People smiled and politely clapped when he was through, some wondering if Billy Joel was right. Looking at my grandmother, I wondered if only *the cursed live long*. I imagine a couple of other families in the room wondered the same thing. An angry looking 40ish woman got up for the second song of the contest. A screeching, furiously delivered rendition of the Bee-Gees *Staying Alive*, almost as a direct protest to Billy Joel. I was shocked to discover that I was in the midst of a political debate wrapped in a cloak of karaoke. If only all debates were fought this way.

I decided to have a little fun and go next. I got up, took the microphone from the right-wing Bee Gee nut, made my selection, and ambitiously began singing *Homeward Bound* by Simon and Garfunkel. I started off pretty well, as least I thought. "Every day is an endless dream of cigarettes and magazines . . . I wish I was homeward bound." I was in the zone for about half the song when I caught a glimpse of the right-wing Bee Gee lady. Her eyebrows were furrowed and she was staring me down. I thought more about what she could have possible been thinking and lost my own place in the process. Caught in a stare-down, I felt uncomfortable and, without the TV, forgot the rest of the lyrics. I laughed into the mic and expected at least a round of applause, but got something rather different.

"BOOOOOOOOOOOOOO!" screamed Right-wing Bee Gee.

I laughed a little to myself again, again wondering what this nut was thinking.

"BOOOOOOOOOOOOOO!"

The rest of the attendees at the party looked on in bewilderment. This was a daughter, not a resident, so it ran out of the jurisdiction of the nurses. I was on my own.

"Can I help you ma'am?"

"How dare you make fun of these people!? Do you think it's funny that they can't remember things? What kind of sick fuck are you?" she softly screamed at me.

I continued speaking into the microphone as if I were a president answering questions from an audience. This must be how he feels.

"What are you talking about?" I responded, somewhat cluelessly.

"The song. You pretending to forget the lyrics. What do you think I am, some kind of idiot?"

It was becoming quite clear that she was.

"You should be ashamed of yourself for making fun of these people. They are beautiful people . . . they are people."

The Bee Gees nut began to cry. I didn't fight back, I just stood up there and let her get out what she needed to get out. The rest of the party trickled out of the room and back to their privacy. I later found out that the nut wasn't really a nut. It turned out that her mother had just recently been placed in the home and this woman, her daughter, was having a very hard time dealing with it. I can't say I didn't understand. Maybe she was worried about what lay in store for her. Maybe she was coping with what was, in essence, the loss of her mother.

We drove home from the Home the same way as always: in silence. Thinking about the woman at the party, it stirkes me as somewhat amazing that everyone deals with things in different ways. Nearly without fail, the car rides home found my aunt softly crying in the front seat until her tears run dry. My uncle chain-smoked his cigarettes and stared straight at the road, never once consoling or even looking at his inconsolable wife. My cousin listened to a boyband on her portable CD player, finding escape in their absurdity. Me? I tend to just sit and think, gathering my thoughts to eventually write something like this.

It always felt like a shorter trip on the way home.

Hinting at Pleasures

Fragrance released with the slice of a knife
against flesh, pale juice splashes on my palm;
I lick the soft center, across life-line,
love-line to thumb-tip. Wine-reminiscent
flavors pique the morning and kiss my lips.

Soft skin, each half is placed in a white bowl.
Serrated edge slips in between the pulp
and skin, blade severs connective tissue,
each tiny sac shifts, some split and spill out,
others hold fast. Sweet/tart, one sip tells all.

Eyes closed, the sauvignon blanc finishes
where the pinot grigio began, hinting
at pleasures of an evening yet to come
begun with a morning of fresh grapefruit.

Siobhan

WINE ABOUT IT

It's only life and morning. Nothing to
get bent about . . . Grapefruit and oatmeal;
when did we get this old? Who's old? Not us,
we still know: how to stay up late and watch
celluloid classics; to sip the right wine —
whatever wine we like at the moment —
how to neck on the couch (without getting
caught); how to smile at butterflies; how to
appreciate the trilling of birds trying
to call up spring from the phoenix-ashes
of winter's cold hearth. So things have changed some —
we've learned to describe fruit in terms of wine,
what nose, what body, what front and palate . . .
Morning is made for fruit, evening for wine.

David M Pitchford

NOTHING BUT TIME

It bangs against windows, screams to get out,
slips quietly between cracks in a life
falling apart, being blown down the street,
random acts of kindness unable to
hold it together long enough to heal.

In a calm moment, it yawns alongside
lethargy/apathy, partners in this
crime. Is failure to function an excuse?
Rationale for the unreasonable?
Or simply the current state of being?

Where the two roads meet, a vacancy sign
proclaiming space enough for one or two
fills the emptiness that stretches beyond
sight and I can see nothing but time waits.

Siobhan

Time Waits

for nothing. It shoves past, locomotive
in intensity and habit — now fast,
then slow, always inexorable as
our next breath . . . and then some! Time, substantive
in its insubstant ubiquity, shall last
beyond everything known, already has

it pushed beyond what was known, what we knew
to be reality; force that it is,
Time changed everything formerly held true
by our youth and younger selves; see it whiz
past only in the rearview — whom moves who
to pass beyond this day — the way it is . . .

Time waits for nothing, for none, but passes
us as we kill it with slow, dragging asses.

David M Pitchford

SHOVELING SNOW

I never once thought of Buddha today
as I shoveled six metric tons of snow
from the drive, opening a channel to
the street. I thought of nothing. *Mu*. What is
that the state of emptiness related
to action as opposed to thought? I'm no
Buddhist, don't play one on TV or in
poems or writs or otherwise; but then,
I guess there is something to vacancy
of thought and the simple purity of
action. Of course, now that I sit inside
and think of it, I think of Collins as
my bodhisattva of snow-shoveling
and sonneteering. If such things exist . . .

David M Pitchford

If Such Things Exist . . .

I exist. This simple fact shouts in pain
radiating from lower back down legs
whose muscles have been put to little use
until this day of snow piled up against
our lives, leaving us very little choice
but to man-handle it out of our way
mixing with pieces of our broken breath.

I think. Try as I might to not be here
in this moment, the reality is
too strong to ignore — I know that I am.

Swirls within the vacancy of thought curl
around present circumstances, bring me
close to recognizing the benefits
found from losing one's self beneath the snow.

Siobhan

ARNOUX TRAV: VICTORY AT XANDR-DIN

David M Pitchford

Viscindi Galwa spat over the high, stone-block wall of Xandr-Din. His eyes narrowed as he gazed into the distance in the waxing sunlight of day's prime. Two armies besieged the ancient city. The third Primus Keinwhid of the Lands of Sunset had brought his son for his first blooding. Xerxes Vace, the second emperor of Maltopia who had named himself after his favorite legendary monarch, marched his armies opposite the Keinwhid forces, Maneguard clustered strategically on his front lines.

"Bring him," Galwa ordered a young monk in a cinnamon colored smock. The young monk glided swiftly away.

† † †

"Why the boy?" asked Badru Ibn Abbas, Prince of Xandr-Din. "I am the general of my armies. I shall ride my chariot out under the shining rays of Amen-Ra and reclaim the splendor and glory of my ancestors."

"You are welcome to your foolishness," Galwa replied. "If you so choose."

"What auguries?" Badru asked the aged priest, wondering again how a withered, diminutive man could hold such personal presence. Even Badru's father, Abbas Ibn Sayyid, had not been as imposing.

"The falcon flew south, the dove huddles in her cage, and Ra promised blood in the dawning," Galwa said calmly. "Dawn's kid bleated on the altar; its gall bladder was filled with stones and the artery of its heart was curved backward. Its brain was enlarged but perfect."

A tall, hooded figure in a grey robe approached in respectful silence and bowed to each in turn.

"Prince Badru Ibn Abbas," Galwa motioned to the cloaked figure. "This is he, Arnoux Trav."

"My dear Trav," Badru bowed. "It is my great pleasure to meet you. Great and many have been the words of praise I have heard from my friend, Viscindi Galwa. May it please the gods you are equal to the task he has brought to test you."

Trav bowed politely. Badru recoiled in shock at the other's silence and looked to Galwa, Teacher of the Mikari.

"He has taken an oath of silence . . ." Galwa began.

"How can a mute save my city! Camel dung! I have had enough of foolishness!" He turned and gave orders for his army to assemble behind the gates.

Galwa turned back to watch the troop progressions in the fields facing the city. "Take this lesson to heart, Trav. Gaze out now and note the troops, their arrangements, the way they spread to cover their weakness and show strength. Think how you will exploit their softness, turn their power against them, and win from them their victory."

Trav pulled the hood back to improve his field of vision. His shaven pate brought a sense of timeless youth to his hard-angled face. Blue-grey eyes gazed placidly out of a serene, seeming untouchable countenance to take in the scene below.

Down at the gate, Badru rallied his troops and arranged them for a sally against the Keinwhid forces. He commanded his lancers to attack Keinwhid's cavalry, the Koenigsguard, his mounted archers to ready themselves to rain hell into the flank closest to the Maltopian Maneguard. Twelve-thousand lightly armored militia footmen were commanded to hold the main gate, leaving only volunteer militia to defend the city should the gate be breached—that and the 600 Mikari monks Viscindi Galwa had committed to the defense of Xandr-Din.

"Should the city fall," Galwa said mildly to Arnoux Trav, the gray-robed warrior, "we are here to assure it falls to Keinwhid and not these savage *Katchka*." He used the race name for the brutal peoples that comprised most of the Maltopian Empire.

Trav motioned to the other, weaving his hands swiftly in a language only used by the Mikari elite.

"Speak," Galwa said. "Your Vow is fulfilled. You must now leave this life and take on the one appointed."

"Yes," Trav said, his voice a husky whisper unused for seven years. "I thank my teacher. These lines are wise, yet unwily. Keinwhid is too cautious, Vace of the *Katchka* overconfident."

"Then you have formed a strategy?"

"Many," Trav nodded, watching and plotting even as he conversed with his mentor.

"Questions cloud your aura, young son," Galwa commented.

"I am young," he kept his eyes on the activity below. "Unblooded as that prince of Keinwhid . . ."

"And yet wiser than either general," Galwa nodded. "You have studied seven years the histories, the philosophers, the scriptures of civilizations long gone to the dust of memory. You are well prepared—and though unblooded, not untested."

"Say your will," Trav bowed. "I am but a tool in the broad hand of providence."

"Tools are only as useful as those who wield them," Galwa stated the axiom in chanted tonality.

"I am the will and the guide of providence," Trav set his jaw, inhaling deeply to calm his mind. "What outcome do you desire, Teacher?"

"Let the Orbs roll their dice," Galwa sang again in axiom. "Ashur has no love of learning; he fears rebellion should his hordes learn their own ignorance. Should he win Xandr-Din, the library and temples of art shall be destroyed by fire and ignorant superstition.

"I forbid that should happen. We care not otherwise who is victor—nor whom vanquished."

Trav signaled for an acolyte, ordering the Mikari to the walls. He had them station themselves as closely as possible to each other to provide cover fire with their slings. Though the slings were ideal for the mountain campaigns the Mikari normally participated in, Trav was certain the height of the wall would help to make them as formidable as the bows below. His orders were simple: *prevent any outsider from entering.*

He watched as the gate opened to emit a host of horsemen as Badru charged out to form lines. Xandr-Din's army fanned out as if to face both armies, stretching from the unscalable Cliff of the Sun on the north to the Butte of Gods, an extinct volcano, to the south. These natural fortifications had proven horribly effective for time immemorial, just as the western rear of the city was protected by the desert of Jyne Din's nagas, serpents that swam the desert like eels, feeding on everything that came to the sand.

Trav thought on the mystery of the serpents as he watched the three armies shift like swirling tides of metallic shallows. Xandr-Din had been built in the ancient times of colossal builders, crafty men whose sole endeavor was conquest for the sake of creating immortal icons to themselves. From these ancients had risen the pyramids, the sphinx, the World Wall in the east, the grand temples of Nassus at Troy, Aarnia, Jericho,

Jerusalem, other ancient settlements—and this immortal city with its temples, libraries, and immense defenses said to have been raised with godly might by Jyne Din himself and his thirteen concubines, the Nagadanites.

Despite his reverie, Trav noted with wry satisfaction that both besieging armies continued to form ranks such that they were best defended from each other's treachery. Trav's predictions formed before his eyes just as they had in his imagination. He looked on in stony silence, internally adjusting the details of his strategy to fit reality while searching his mind for the lore that would lead him to victory.

Jyne Din had built a double gate in the west to prevent the nomadic tribes from approaching via the desert. Legends long since ancient told of a mighty prince who had gathered the tribes together and attacked the city out of desperation in a seven-year famine. Jyne Din had been pierced with the prince's sword, and saved himself by using his sorcery to meld himself with the prince to become a colossus of salt. The supposed colossus now sat in an ornate throne in the great Palace, which was forbidden to all but the highest, noblest persons—those to pass the test of Jariddne Din. Three men in history had passed the test, though legend claimed others.

Trav veiled his mind in Mikari discipline, keeping hidden his secret knowledge of the nagas.

Silence slammed down on the plains of Xandr-Din. Three armies faced each other, motionless, from distances comfortably safe from bowshot. A champion stepped out from each and cast his javelin in the ancient tradition. Parties from each rode out to meet in the triangle of land bordered by the javelins.

"Terms!" Badru barked.

"Keinwhid offers life and liberty to all who concede," said Primus Keinwhid.

"How kind," Badru said dryly, his lips curling in a snarl of contempt.

"Xerxes offers swifter death in his inestimable mercy," offered the dark emperor. His eyes broiled with hatred, malice and ambition enough to send a shiver of anticipation through the whole group.

"Another magnanimous offer," Badru said, this time in soft scorn.

"What terms offers the glorious and terrible Badru Ibn Abbas Ibn Sayyid Ibn Din?" Keinwhid bowed, his voice toned for calculated diplomacy.

"To Keinwhid," Badru smiled and bowed in the manner of his people, "I offer one fresh horse from my own stable and leave to retire to his own kingdom—having remunerated the lands and people of Din Aashra.

"To Vace," his eyes flashed menace, "withdrawal in full and I shall require only a trifle to repay abuses to my peoples—the life of Vace, Usurper of the *Katchka*!"

"We are agreed then," Xerxes Vace drew his sword and saluted. Keinwhid looked with admiration at the dark emperor's sword, Angra Mainyu, and drew his own broad, two-edged blade in marshal salute as did Badru with his slight but swift scimitar. They moved to join their respective armies and await what promised to be the monumental battle of the age.

† † †

"Tell me of the blade Angra Mainyu," Trav said quietly, respectfully to Viscindi Galwa.

"What is to tell? It is a sliver of metal beaten by a smith, honed to severing sharpness, and soaked in the blood of heroes and villains."

"It lives," Trav stated dully. His eyes remained on the unfolding events in the field. The ranks of soldiers, horses and others moiled into final preparations, their commanders stoically poised to lead them into battle.

"Angra Mainyu is a demon," Galwa said neutrally. "It is said that the demon possessed a smithy in the time celestials roamed the earth. Through the masterful skill of the smithy, Mainyu forged the sword to perfection. Taking it up, he struck down the nine sons of Bishma-Tizaree and Hymnia-Sylth, princes and godlings all. In his revenge, Bishma sought to destroy the blade along with the demon, but Hymnia sang the sacred Lyric of Bondage and bound Mainyu's spirit into the sword itself and hid it for another age to find . . ."

Trav pondered the story for a time while the armies below came to a standstill and anticipated the coming battle. Thunder rumbled from the south where clouds had begun to gather as though to witness some spectacle. Dust settled across the plain under a harsh sun grown hot in the later throes of spring. Trav felt the calm creep along his nerves like a breath held in anticipation of meeting The Maker.

"Today shall matter little in this conflict," he pronounced, defying the instinct toward awe.

† † †

From the hour following until the sun sat like a fiery egg nested in the city's western heights, the armies swirled and bucked and strew death and injury over the plain before the gates of Xandr-Din. Though the separate leaders strove with great might toward each other, the armies rallied time and again to throw back the attacks of their foes. As the city's shadow began to pool like blood seeping from its walls onto the field, Badru Din called the remnant of his army back into the gates.

† † †

"Three thousand? In one day's battles? How can this be?" Badru's scratched but freshly cleaned face shone pale in the lamplight of his council chamber.

"It is so," Galwa reported calmly. "Keinwhid lost fewer, Vace many times more."

"Yes," Badru protested, "but that evil blade, Angra Mainyu, took no fewer than five-hundred of my best horsemen! How can such as this be defeated?!"

"Do you ask my council? Or rave 'gainst the gods?" Galwa asked nonchalantly.

"Yes!" Badru spat. "Yes! Damn you. Impart to me some wisdom with which to defeat my enemy."

"You must first rule yourself," Galwa said, his eyes catching the lamplight in an odd flash.

"I shall have you flayed," Badru clenched his jaw, biting the words one at a time.

"Flay me if you wish," Galwa shrugged. "It would not be the wise course of action. But now I choose to take offense and recognize that you and I have lost respect of each other. Therefore should you seek counsel elsewhere."

Galwa walked from the room unswerving and unassailed. Though Badru motioned the guards to detain the ancient Master, they found themselves unwilling to carry out Badru's will.

"Fetch his mute!" Badru raved at them.

"I am here," Arnoux Trav made his entrance.

Badru's eyes widened in surprise, though no trace of anything but rage shone in his countenance. Trav had changed from his pilgrim robes to a suit of armor Galwa had requisitioned from a local craftsman. A brushed steel breastplate topped his fine chain tabard, his hips and legs were plated appropriately for cavalry, and he carried a sheathed sword buckled neatly at his left hip. The sword's hilt was plainly polished bone or ivory, as was the hilt of the matching dagger sheathed on Trav's right thigh.

"You," Badru arched his eyebrows. "You have broken with the priests?"

"I am no longer a monk," Trav bowed. "Your highness, Badru ibn Din, I am Arnoux Trav, Fatefist of the Mikari."

"Well met!" Badru smiled gleefully. He'd been raised on stories of the ancient order of Mikari Fatefists. Reputed as the greatest warriors in the world, each was marked for it from the time they were left on the steps of any Mikari academy. It had been a hundred years since anyone had been chosen—most surmised this to be a result of the Mikari falling out of fashion and dwindling in number.

"Do you place your army in my hands?" Trav asked, looking the monarch in the eye unflinching.

"By no means," Badru smiled. "Nevertheless, my heart praises the Lord of my ancestors for blessing the sons of Din with such a tool."

"What do you wish of me?"

"You," Badru paused momentarily, his brow furrowing. "You shall be my Flank and keep my life."

"So be it," Trav bowed, intoning the ritual acquiescence, "so is it, so shall it be."

"What action suggest you for the morrow?" Badru's eyes shone.

"None," Trav said decisively.

"None!" Badru looked to the guard. "Do you hear? The Fatefist would have us idle away our time while Keinwhid and Vace decide which portions of my city to possess."

"Xandr-Din shall fall to no foe," Trav stated flatly.

"How can I defeat my foes from the craven's post?!"

"They shall grow restless and turn upon each other in the manner of scavengers." Trav pointed to the map rolled out between them on a large cedar table. "Keinwhid has his army at hand. Vace is not so unwise; despite his superior numbers, he has left substantial reinforcement back at the fords of the Godsblood. That force is nearly equal in number to Keinwhid's as it stands."

Badru staggered under the weight of this revelation. "You tell me Vace has another third of his army—another thirty-thousand in the Waterhorse plains?"

"It is so," Trav nodded. "I took count when passing . . ."

"Gods of the desert! Gods of the plains!" Badru spat as he screamed his frustration. He cursed vociferously several minutes before taking a deep breath. "You pronounce my defeat."

"I report your challenge," Trav shrugged.

"How old are you, boy?" Badru glared at him hotly.

"I was brought to Mikari-Jedra nineteen years ago," Trav answered flatly.

"By your age," Badru moved in close enough for Trav to smell the peppers and clove on his breath. "By your age, I had killed four-hundred bandits, led two campaigns against the infidel armies, and sired three sons."

"I have not accomplished as much, emir," Trav looked him steadily in the eye. Though the pale foreigner was much taller than the prince, he was nearly as trim. Each bore himself with the confidence of royalty, one from the confidence of his birth, the other from the confidence of self discipline.

Badru's eyes flashed dangerously, then he forced out a loud, raucous guffaw.

"You have a spirit of iron, boy," Badru slapped his shoulder. "Be wise enough to never again challenge me in my own city. I am ruler here. Keep it in mind."

"Thank you, emir, for the sage advice," Trav bowed ceremoniously. "Have you further desire of my counsel this night?"

"Yes," Badru snapped. "Advise me as to how I may wreak havoc on my enemy—without hiding behind the monuments of my esteemed and most worshipful ancestors."

"Let the Mikari stand as they did today, holding at bay with their slings all too eager to await your invitation," Trav began. "In your endless generosity, grant them the morning to grow curious. Once the sun has risen beyond its blinding rise, let the desert's heat assault their courage and sap their strength while your armies bathe and oil themselves in the city's luxury."

"This seems . . ." Badru opened his hands and then spread his arms wide.

"Once the sun has dropped to first bleed shadow from the city's wall," Trav continued, "bring all your horsemen against the border of the two armies like a wedge. Drive in with vengeful fury and howling to wake the sands. Then, just as quickly, turn and flee like a fox with his tail afire. The armies will close on you and each other, and there each of your warriors acts as three by drawing the foes . . ."

"Aha!" Badru clapped his hands. "Masterful!"

Understanding that he was dismissed, Trav bowed and made his way out to find Viscindi Galwa.

☦ ☦ ☦

"He is unwise," Trav told his mentor. "He is impatient."

"Why?" Galwa asked.

"He is made small by the greatness of his ancestors." Trav thought on it. "That is, he perceives himself such and strives to greater glory. Saving Xandr-Din is secondary to reaping personal glory. He wishes to be the hero, but fears his fate is otherwise."

"Yet, he has some measure of wisdom, does he not?" Galwa sat in a meditative trance. Though Trav was accustomed to this from a lifetime of association with the Mikari Master, others looking in would have been confounded to understand how the statuesque man could speak without moving.

"He does," Trav conceded after a moment.

"What wisdom has he shown?"

"He did not linger in the field as a more rash man might have," Trav said, searching his own thoughts. "Perhaps he is more wily than wise; and yet this is a sort of wisdom. He has insight into the souls of men such that he may lead or control . . ."

"And?"

Trav mulled the thought. Galwa's candles burned down nearly an inch before he spoke again. "He has put his trust in you, my Teacher."

"No, Arnoux Trav," Galwa said sagely. "The emir has put his trust in you—and the reputation of the Mikari Fatefists. Shows he proper respect?"

"Badru respects little," Trav gazed into the fading flames of his mentor's candles. "Badru loves only Badru and all he envisions himself to accomplish."

"How does this serve our purpose, Fatefist?"

"Badru's unreasoned quest for glory is a flame in the fire of our torch," Trav intoned to the candle flame, visions of battles and strategies forming like mist beneath the placid glaze of his eyes. "He shows wisdom also in this, that he commanded that I should be his shield and Flank."

"You assented to this?" Galwa inflected the statement so slightly that only someone very familiar with him would recognize its implications. Still, he seemed motionless, suspended by invisible strings.

"He wishes to test my mettle," a flicker like a sudden smile flashed across Trav's face, hinting at youth and hard-edged handsome features. His smoky blue eyes narrowed at the corners subtly. "Having seen the Dance of a Thousand Strokes in tomorrow's battles, he will grow ambitious and change directives."

"Perhaps," Galwa dismissed him.

† † †

Trav's gelding stamped impatiently beside the emir's stallion. Though the afternoon had grown hot in the still air, Trav remained unperturbed. He cooed to his horse by name, Tabanyor, and prepared his mind for what was to follow. Something like an excited thrill ran deep through his heart though no thought or emotion shown on his marble features.

"It is time," Badru growled.

"No," Trav replied in a low, toneless voice. "At the whistle of Mikari slings . . ."

"I command here," Badru bit out the words.

"As you choose, emir," Trav nodded slightly in respectful acquiescence.

One thousand horsemen waited behind them—one hundred with long spears, behind them two hundred with drawn scimitars, behind them five hundred with the famed Aashran bow, followed by the remaining lines alternating lancers and swordsmen.

"Command the gate!" Badru told the stony youth. Trav did as ordered.

"Command the march!" It began.

† † †

Trav launched himself into the path of four Maneguard as they bore down on the emir. His mind noted but dismissed the intense messages from his nerves—exhaustion was easily overcome by the discipline of Mikari training. For the thousandth time today he raised his heavy blade and arced it down with deadly intent upon the enemy.

Despite his respect for their reputation, Trav was surprised and impressed with the Maneguard. They were well armored, but more than that they knew how to use their armor—knew how to shift minutely, and with an economy of motion to conserve strength while absorbing blows. No other group of warriors on the field had fared so well against him. No other now moved within reach of the deadly Fatefist.

Trav let the weakest of the four past him, allowing others to assist in the emir's defense. He shifted to bring a broad swing down toward the strongest of the Mane, but curved the stroke an inch from the knight's upraised shield and diverted the momentum to a sweeping backhand slash at the Mane closing on his right. Steel blade bit through iron plates to shatter that knight's collarbone and slice deep into his throat as he left himself exposed in what he'd thought was a sure deathblow against the monk.

Hooves came down on Trav's shield as a knight risked his horse in a rearing attempt to unsaddle the Mikari Fatefist. Trav let his left shoulder relax to absorb the blow while tensing his right and bending forward at the waist to push the horse aside. The horse stumbled, its rider disengaging fluidly, unharmed as only a Maneguard could.

"Badru falls! Defend! Defend!"

Trav dropped from his horse as gracefully, perhaps even more fluidly than the Maneguard. He spun and leaped in a series of attacks that took him to Badru's side.

"I bade you defend me!" the wild-eyed, furious emir screamed.

"You remain unscathed," Trav's voice was hoarse. He realized for the first time that he had been shouting and screaming throughout the hours of combat. His detached self noted the clear sky darkening with the shadows of late afternoon. He killed four more warriors with a series of blows and then scanned the field.

Emir Badru's personal bodyguards had dwindled in number from two dozen to nine still standing. Each was exhausted, barely able to stand when not directly engaged. Though the lines were well-formed for the time they'd spent in combat, Trav could see that most of the forces were exhausted from the day's heavy engagement. Blood flowed across the plain, a mist of it seemed to rise with the dust from horizon to horizon. The dead and wounded lay in a chaos of heaps and clusters interspersed with the mayhem of ongoing battle.

"Sound the horn: withdrawal!"

"I have not begun to tire!" Badru raved savagely. "I shall drive every Daeva, druj, and yatu from this land and into the abyss of Asha's vengeance!"

Trav dropped the final Maneguard within reach of them and turned to the emir's bodyguard Dupda ibn Ghadja, "Blow your horn."

Dupda nodded his head slightly and reached within his dun colored robes for the horn. He pulled it free as another group of enemy soldiers approached, this time Keinwhid forces.

"I forbid you!" Badru's eyes flashed madness, the pulse at his temple throbbing like a threat of divine rage.

"Nevertheless," Trav snatched the horn from Dupda's hand and blew three series of short bursts to signal an ordered withdrawal.

"Impudent . . ." Badru attacked him.

Trav took a quick step to his right and pulled the scimitar from Badru's grasp. Part of his mind worked on the problem of the advancing enemy.

"Impossible!" Badru gaped, wide-eyed and disbelieving, at his own weapon in Trav's hand. "That is a blessed weapon; divine will holds it to my hand—none may disarm me. . ."

"Yet it is so," Trav said calmly, tossing the blade back to its owner and turning to face the oncoming threat of Keinwhid's knights.

He held up his hand, "I challenge you to the Rite of Masters."

Keinwhid's knights stopped. The lesser soldiers stepped back to let them pass. One disengaged from the rest.

"Your terms?" asked the knight, raising his mesh visor. Trav noted the silver coronet artfully worked into the knight's helm. His shield was emblazoned with the Keinwhid dragon.

"The day is tired," Trav said. "And gorged on the blood of heroes. Let us decide today's balance. Each shall retire with his men to his respective place and disengage from battle with the other."

"So let it be," Keinwhid the younger nodded, smiling. "I am the son of Keinwhid; who, may I say, was fool enough to challenge me?"

"You do not share your sire's caution," Trav observed. "I am Arnoux Trav, Fatefist of the Mikari and lately guarantor of Badru ibn Abbas and the sovereignty of Xandr-Din."

The two champions saluted each other with their swords and began an intricate dance of martial triumph. They seemed almost choreographed as they stepped, lunged, and whirled around, toward, then away from each other. Their swords flashed and sang with innumerable strokes and ripostes.

"You know the Dance of a Thousand Strokes," Trav smiled.

"Yes," said Keinwhid the Younger. "I have studied many lores of the sword."

Crowds grew around them as exhausted soldiers and knights broke off from their battles to watch the spectacle of the prince and priest. Their fluid dance, seemingly unencumbered by the plates and coats of armor each man wore, mesmerized the watching warriors. Silence spread from the circle as the number of onlookers grew and word spread throughout the ranks.

"Cease this travesty," a low, thunderous voice cut through the ringing song of the swords and the low mutter of the crowd's appraisal. Xerxes Vace stepped out of the crowd, the crowd having fallen away from the threat of his dark, blood-covered blade, Angra Mainyu.

Trav brushed off a powerful slash and disengaged, his placid battle smile turning to a disgruntled frown, then to a placid mask of marble invulnerability. He stepped back from Keinwhid the Younger, opened his left hand and pointed his sword at the ground in a gesture of disengagement.

Keinwhid the Younger sheathed his sword in a blurred motion and lifted his visor. Trav noted now that the prince was no older than himself. Keinwhid the Younger was flushed from the exertion of their battle; sweat streamed down his face and his breath was ragged with strain.

"You have no right to the Contest of Champions on a field of three armies," Xerxes glared at them contemptuously. "Or have you formed an alliance against me?"

"Perhaps," Trav said quietly, willing his own breathing to calm. "Perhaps we are even now deciding that."

"I suppose," interjected a voice from the Keinwhid side of the circle, "that this could be decided presently."

Keinwhid the Elder stepped into the circle and made polite gestures to respective commanders. "To my ears, *Katchka* king," he growled in a low baritone, "that rings of challenge. Is it your wish that the fate of this siege be here and now decided?"

Vace smiled. Knights and warriors trembled and pushed against each other to give the tyrant—and themselves—more space. Vace stepped into the circle and threw his helm to the ground, whirling his infamous blade above his head with a sound like locusts swarming.

"I shall eat your heart, Keinwhid," he bared his teeth in an expression that could never be called a smile. "And you, False-fate of the pumpkin robes—I shall eat your eyes."

"And what would you have from Xandr-Din?" Badru stepped in, his eyes smoldering, the point of his scimitar weaving figure-eights in a lazy rhythm.

"There is no part of Badru *ibn ibn ibn* Din worthy of eating," Xerxes Vace spat in reply.

"We have our terms, then?" Keinwhid the Younger had caught his breath for the most part. He stepped forward brazenly, though Trav could read uncertainty behind his defiant eyes, belying the rigid intrepidation of his stance.

"These terms," Trav stepped in. "We shall strive against each other. The last standing shall have his terms. Name them now."

"My terms are the surrender of all to me," Vace seemed somehow to shadow the sun itself in his assertion. "Khalil, my heir, shall flank me—his terms are my terms."

"My terms are the head of Xerxes Vace and the surrender of Xandr-Din," Keinwhid the Elder said.

"Immediate withdrawal of all troops," Keinwhid the Younger asserted. "I require the head of Xerxes Vace and the shards of his broken sword; of the noble armies of the Mikari and Xandr-Din, I offer the mercy of full service to Keinwhid or immediate, branded exile without return."

"I require the heads of all marshals of the field not allied to Xandr-Din," Badru said darkly. "Enslavement for the footmen, and knights may buy their freedom at one-hundred golden Dinri."

"Xandr-Din and the withdrawal of all persons less their greater arms," Trav said, nodding as though it were already decided.

"By what right!?" Badru fumed. "What right have you as my flank to name your terms?"

"None—as your *Flank*," Trav replied. "I fight for Xandr-Din. I do not serve Badru."

Badru stood shaking for a moment as though given to fits of apoplexy, but then his rage overcame him and he charged the Fatefist. Trav brushed the attack away lightly and turned to face the greater threat of Angra Mainyu in the hands of Xerxes Vace.

Badru gained control of himself with the realization of his situation and used his momentum to engage Keinwhid the Elder. He feinted a direct jab at the king and then spun into a great arcing roundhouse slice powerful enough to decapitate a horse. But Keinwhid was not there when the blow whooshed through empty air. Badru fell to the sand as Keinwhid landed a deft blow with his swordhilt on the back of Badru's head, knocking the emir unconscious.

Keinwhid the Younger began his dance again, this time fighting Khalil. He was only to the fourth thrust of the Dance of a Thousand Strokes when he broke through the young prince's defense and jammed his sword through the scaled armor and into Khalil's left side. When Khalil swung in desperation to avenge the attack, Keinwhid the Younger used a double-fisted cleave with his blade angled and broke the man's arm, deliberately inflicting injury where he could easily have severed the arm.

Trav was on the defensive. He'd begun a variation of the Dance, but Angra Mainyu was ready for it—obviously familiar enough with it to exhaust him. He switched to an ancient dervish style, then through a succession of all the styles he'd been taught and practiced for endless hours. Vace scoffed, cajoling him with every passing flurry of blows. The sword itself seemed to mutter gibberish within his mind, a language he could almost recognize.

Trav began to evolve a style of his own when the Keinwhids joined in against Vace and his cursed blade. In some part of his mind, Trav noted the honorable means by which each had made his way to the current melee. He knew that trained men were even now kneeling to tend the wounds of Badru and Khalil. He did not think anything, but observed it in the high redoubt of his mind.

Vace lunged suddenly away from Trav, sweeping two blades away before slashing in a lightning-fast attack that shattered Keinwhid the Elder's sword and sank into the older king's helmet and head. Blood jetted from the wound and ran down the man's face, into the eyes now glazed with sudden death.

Attack the man, not the sword. The gibberish in Trav's mind suddenly shifted into crystal clarity. Angra Mainyu spoke to him. *Your hand would so much better grip my hilt.* Seductive as only power can be.

Trav batted away a sweeping stroke of Vace's sword and lunged his shoulder into the tyrant's ribs. He spun to meet the returning arc of the enchanted blade, keeping his guard constant and vigilant. Despite Trav's mastery combined with Keinwhid's, Angra Mainyu was drawing ten times more blood and the wounds it inflicted were far worse. Trav's armor was tattered, his robes shredded; Keinwhid had dropped away at some point to discard his breastplate, it being so dented as to encumber him.

Drive in and kill him, Angra Mainyu sang like a siege against Trav's Mikari discipline. *He is no longer worthy. Slay him and set your hand to me. We shall take his empire and spread it tenfold across the earth . . .*

"Silence!" Trav redoubled his efforts, feeling for the first time in several years the weight of his own limbs. His training was so severe that he had grown used to the physical labor of hefting a sword in full armor for the full daylight of any given day. But this was not training. Angra Mainyu hit with far fiercer blows than any before.

Keinwhid went down under the next onslaught. Trav could not tell how badly the young prince was injured, but for the first time on the field he felt—he *felt.* His crystalline redoubt crumbled. Passion gushed like adrenaline throughout his being. He kicked out to stop the killing stroke, striking Vace's left elbow with bone-shattering impact.

"NO!" he screamed. "Honor is the only power I crave!" He pressed his advantage against the *Katchka* tyrant, inventing new series of attacks and defenses as he spent himself against his foe. The gibberish began again within his mind, but he pulled the fire of his passion up to clear the clutter from his soul. He cleansed his mind with the passion's ferocity and poured it like fuel into his will.

Vace spun suddenly into a double-fisted roundhouse and knocked Trav to the ground, his head spinning with impossibilities of unconsciousness. He stared aghast as he realized that Angra Mainyu had changed tactics, had repaired the shattered elbow, and was now on a mission to consume Trav's blood and soul. He rolled to evade the blows.

Near the end of strength, Trav gazed up at the orange glow of Xerxes' sword as it descended unimpeded toward his head. *You are mine . . .*

A blade suddenly intervened, knocking Angra Mainyu aside enough that it bit deep into Trav's left shoulder instead of through his helmet and skull. Trav rolled with the impact and got to his feet, too caught up in sudden hope to acknowledge the timeliness of Keinwhid's intervention.

Three blades flashed in the daylight's dying embers. Sudden bursts of passion ignited in the two sorely wounded young warriors as they faced the older despot with his demon-possessed blade. The blade itself seemed to shimmer toward a climax of hatred and fury. The older man's eyes were vacant, grown vacuous with the full possession of the demon.

Trav spun to knock aside a vicious sweep and came around full into a roundhouse kick to Xerxes' head. Xerxes fell for the first time. The crowd of warriors watching in rapt concentration suddenly cheered. Keinwhid feinted a blow at the fallen king's head, then whipped a slash down on both his wrists. Xerxes' left hand came free, but his right stayed somehow attached and clutched to the sword.

Comprehension dawned on Trav as he watched Vace bring his stump together with the severed hand in a bright orange flash. His hands were whole once more. Trav lunged, twirled and suddenly held two swords. Keinwhid sprawled toward the crowd's edge. The crowd gasped in mixed awe and trepidation.

Xerxes Vace, maniacal grimace now painting his features with madness and demonic glee, charged at Trav and spun a net of steel around him. Trav worked both blades with equal alacrity, though the strength of his blows suffered and the pain in his left shoulder robbed him of his usual martial grace. He wove a net to counter Angra Mainyu's—spinning, ducking, dodging and tumbling like some manic acrobat. It had all come down to a moment's decision of survival.

Finally, Trav found his opening. His mind wrapped around the sequence of the demon's attack; he understood its strategy. He dodged a brilliant arc and sweep attack, caught the unholy blade on the flat of his left-hand sword and slammed the Mikari sword down with all his might on the blade of Vace's enchanted weapon. The three blades shattered with a bone-jarring shriek and a tinkling like coins on cobblestones.

The final rays of sun passed beyond the horizon. Silence fell like a veil with night's sudden darkness. Trav knelt in the sand, his hands blistered to the elbow as though basted in coals. Xerxes lay still. Keinwhid had risen and now held the emir's scimitar, stooped in a battle stance as though it were impossible that nothing threatened him.

"What will?" Trav croaked through cracked lips.

"What?" Keinwhid the Younger looked around wildly.

"What will?" he repeated.

"This is not my victory," Keinwhid said, shock plain on his features.

"It is," Trav stated flatly.

"No," Keinwhid replied. "I surrender myself."

"You cannot."

"I do," Keinwhid asserted, walking over and pulling his erstwhile foe to his feet. "You have slain our common enemy. The old kings have passed; let us build the kingdoms now in our own image."

"I seek no kingdom," Trav shrugged.

"Then you shall share mine," Keinwhid signaled for someone to tend their wounds. "But then, I guess a Mikari Fatefist has no use for kingdoms."

"You guess correctly," Viscindi Galwa came forward from the crowd of watchers. "A Mikari Fatefist has no use of a kingdom. However, Arnoux Trav has sufficed in his service; I release him to his own."

Galwa strode to Trav and took the young man's hands tenderly, carefully in his own. He bent his head forward and muttered several prayers. Their hands glowed swirls of iridescent blues and greens as Trav closed his eyes and breathed his way into familiar trance.

Have I shamed you, Master? Trav sent his voice timidly into their internal melding of light.

Shame is not for the enlightened, Trav was cushioned in pillows of blue luminescence and a silvery mantra of healing.

† † †

Usurper: Self-Transplanted Fern of God

David M Pitchford

He was a scholar made—born to nothing
save maybe the slow rotting southern night
under Arkansas skies. He read for want
of escape—from reality with its
biting lash of belt, smother of asthma
braying of the mutts he saw as siblings
though unnatural law had taken them
from one home to another—he read books
to cleanse his soul of clutter, forgive sins
he imagined himself and everyone
to commit. God was his razor-whip, his
personal weapon against loneliness
and 'the thousand natural shocks' life beat
him constantly over the heart with. Life

moved on—north of the Mason/Dixon, line
drawn on a map meaning nothing to him.
Junior high school and another new tongue
he must split from the tinge, the tang of drawl
whipped into his spirit like the habit
of prayer that kept his pitch soul safe each night
under the protective palm of that god
who so often lashed the earth with vengeance
in anger so violent lightening itself
quaked fear in dreams of His presence—
forget forgiveness, vengeance is the Lord's!
A good Christian boy, he read his Bible,
read the Psalms, Proverbs, gospels, epistles—
studied till his heart convicted his soul,

condemned it for spiritual adultery
at only fifteen years old—sentenced him
to Hell for eternity on the stain
of hatred clouding his every motive . . .
But reason crept in, usurped the gavel,
tapped three times on Judgement's temple, then laughed

in the Accuser's face. No. Truth is greater
than judgement, is greater than stone-written
laws—vengeance is the Fool's! Is God not Love?
Love defends, love heals, love hopes, love bends, love
gives without breaking, breaks without failing,
love lies for its own sake, love steals for need,
love answers and questions and pushes past
to meet Truth in Eden's Garden, where God

faces his own reflection to learn more
what He is, is not. He studies, searching
all things to find Truth, which is Him, unknown
yet knowing all things, all times . . . Learning for
the sake of knowing, and because searching,
growing, learning—these are life. And His own

life unfolds among the cosmos, reaches
and breeches eternity's null borders,
penetrates outer darkness—where not exist
possibilities of void, nothing, null—
he reads of oceans, dreams of white beeches
where life is simpler, where no word-mortars
assault defenses deep embedded—*Resist
perfection; in eternal search is life full* . . .

Pushing forty, he turns to look behind—
echoes of salt pillars shadow his mind,

but he brightens his own little lamp, turns
up the volume on a syncopated
song and smiles as he feels the nothing—burns
leave scars to armor nerves—sins he hated
in youth he disbelieves, become now mere
dysfunction with rational cures—*The flesh
is weak, but the spirit prevails*—his truth
came of age slow molting, snakelike, his youth—
irrepressible as life . . . something fresh,
something like wisdom, something far yet near

to inspiration he takes now for granted,
usurps fortune and thrives where he was not planted.

Once a fern of God, he has transplanted
himself in friendlier arbors. He smiles
seldom as Midwestern calms, prairie winds
blowing grasses that sway his sundry moods,
bending reeds as though in some sacred dance
of punitive justice—lash! jump! scream! lash!
Respect is a fickle thing—with one lash
a wild tongue may unroot though it's planted
deep in fertile ground. Beyond its one dance,
respect has no legs to carry . . . He smiles
hollow as scarecrows to those whose dark moods
come vociferous, venomous as winds
from Hell's dark desolation. Such foul winds
from ego of the Narcissist may lash
his eyes of a dark hour, but better moods
and Reason shield him. No good root planted
in good soil bears bad fruit—decadence smiles
at the lie; fruit and time go bad one dance
at a time—when fates with fortunes dance
nothing is left to the fickle choice of winds
to declare. He knows; he grows; he thin smiles
at forces still playing on his soul—lash
out as he will, he knows no names . . . Planted
within the earth, he is subject to moods
of orbs, gravities unnamable, to moods
changed by distant stars and their cosmic dance
around the maypole ancient gods planted
at Eternity's end/begin. By winds
we're borne like brave Ulysses, forced to lash
ourselves 'gainst siren song and shine our smiles
wily toward home, forging on, granting smiles
to meaner gods of ungenerous moods
who in their petty anger take to lash
us like temple merchants—and yet we dance
our own tunes. Plug our ears. Brace against winds
that try to uproot us where we're planted.

Like brave Ulysses, he his chosen dance
dances to usurp other powers—winds
that bend, but leave him still, self-transplanted.

GATES OF ARCADIA

David M Pitchford

Lo! We have gathered at the fallen wall of Jericho. Mourn, ye mourners; wail ye weeping women! For Arcadia is fallen, her gates but rubble at the feet of barbarian hordes! Here shall be much weeping, gnashing of teeth, bitter tears shed, and prayers for mercy! Here shall be psalms composed on the broken heartstrings of minstrels yet unborn; here shall be erected no monument but the desolate cry in an unheard wilderness!

Okay, so maybe the resignation of our previous Spec. Fiction editor is not so momentous as all that . . . Have no fear; *Prism* is strong—it will survive. And the current editors continue to love the fiction submitted by eager writers of all genres, including a special fondness for Fantasy and Spec. Fiction.

Please feel free to write in or email and tell us what you think—and while you're at it, send us fiction to consider.

Meanwhile, enjoy the rich tapestry of verse and prose woven into these final pages. An old favorite from several issues back, our pirate-voiced contributor James Princeton Garr gives us his dragonized rendition of Coleridge's *Rime of the Ancient Mariner*. Prolific author Christopher Heath shares one of over fifty of his *Azieran* tales. Cheryl Peugh asks us to decide one way or another in *The Sun or the Moon*. Edward J McFadden, III chills us after that with a heart-warming, while somewhat frightening ontology of Sudden Infant Death Syndrome. And we cap this fat little issue with a chilling tale of apocalypse from the redoubtable Nathan Meyer, to whom I am eternally grateful for this eleventh-hour contribution.

Enjoy the read. Keep your eyes open for future news on the Web: www.prismquarterly.com.

David
March 2007

Dragons Over Sunset Island

James Princeton Garr

Pirates though I captain, heed me now this tale:
of mind sound and body broken, upon this
sliver, this scrap of plane tree snapped by teeth
savager than winter, I come to shore
in this strange land; stranger, heed me. Dragons
over Sunset Island spun their web of calling
and we heard their siren song,
and we heed their siren song;
sixty swarthy souls strong of arm, mind, and will
we sacked the empire's ships for loot and glut,
riches and a harvest of blood. Five years
I led that crew with something akin to
honor as only one wily as legend can,
and I held them in an iron fist of reason
and bought their loyalty
and bought their loyalty
with riches strongarmed from luxuriant galleys.
We shared the best this world has to offer:
wine, women, songs and the sea. Five years
we roamed the five seas under the trine goddess moons
hearing tales of creatures, fantasies of devils,
yarns of monstrous seabeasts and dragons
of every stripe. But never did we believe,
never believe tales of leathern-winged sirens
singing from Sunset Island
from skies above Sunset Island.

Even the isle itself was but fable
to frighten green seamen and lubbers. But these eyes
bear witness to the skydance of dragons
over Sunset Island: something like eastern
crocodiles, like crocodiles but leaner

more sinuous and with wings sail-width,
yes, with wings sinuous and sail-width,
in color like butterflies of the Great Forest,
and with sparkles like the black desert waters.
Stronger than whales harpooned, these creatures
fly, for my first mate in his avarice
did test them, his aim too true for good fortune
as he struck one who ventured closest,
the one that ventured closest, stranger.
Such fury! Never was whale more beastly
in its struggle, dragging the line taut
and pulling our barge like a child's toy. Till sunset
that devil dragged us 'cross the waves under
clear, unwinded sky. Then came his comrades, swooping
down. I tell you stranger, swooping down,
falconish and hungry as angry like hornets
on a foolish boy. Swooping down they came,
these dragons of Sunset Island, these devils
at sunset's baths. In that first hour of darkness,
neath the Trine, upon the brine calm blue,
swooped they down, swooped they down, swope they down
and sailors died, and sailors died; my crewmen died!
Where the gods of the west lay their fiery heads
to rest, where the Trine sink into the seas
off World's End, where Fire Mountain spews
hatred in the sunset, malice in the sunset.
There did fifty of my crew breathe their final
breath in a rending of flesh in claws cruel
with fury in the rending of flesh,
with fury in the rending of flesh
by teeth cruel with fury
by teeth cruel in malice.

Like the cold-blooded lizards of Gnarl's Candor,
these devils ate meat only from the living,
drank blood in the violence of their hatred
with tongues hollow as reeds and teeth mighty
as the blades of war, mightier than the spears of war.

Only in the belly of our ship, once
the mast was lost with thunderous snaps
and swooping attacks, with thunderous snaps!
we ten did survive night in that savage bay
nestled in sunset island,
lorded over by sunset island.
Three days, till the holy Trine waned empty,
dragons swooped, timbers snapped, sails took flame,
and ten stalwart sailors held council below
Sweet Nagia's decks, cushioned by that soft
surcease only the Vandia's rum can give,
only Vandia's rum does give
nothing but rum can give . . .

On that fourth morning, under cloudless skies
and the Trine sweet slivered, the eastern gods
rose red, and pirates five went up to scout
the fired fields of Sunset Island,
deadly fields of Sunset Island.
Three days and no word returned. Three days
we five who remained conspired escape;
simpler plan no man ever made: we five,
in three skiffs departed under dark of night,
under Trine new waxing
under Trine moons waxing.

Oh barren stars that cursed my crew!
You devil stars! You cursed my crew!
Devil dragons swooped down and we were two.
Dragons swooped and one small bark survived,
and I, captain of the Sweet Nagia,

shamed and beaten fled on this single sliver,
kicking sharks aside now fearless of aught
fearless of aught that in the water dwells,
fearless of aught that from the sky not fells
men to eat their flesh and drink their blood!

A sailor deserves his brine-laden grave.
But currents friendly grabbed this one,
yes currents strangely took this one
as though some freakish god in ire did
want this tale told to all who sail the seas,
want told this tale to all who sail his seas
toward sunset. Oh! Dragons over Sunset Island,
devils who eat the flesh of men and drink their blood.
Sweet Nagia, forgive this gods-abandoned
captain; one day I shall avenge,
one day, by gods, I will avenge!
To vengeance, then! Get me . . .

For vengeance, now, get me fast a new crew
and forfeit your ship to me, stranger. Avast!
With crossbows and harpoons, long spears
and swords flashing, we'll avenge flesh,
avenge the blood of seven times seven
sailors who fed the Dragons over
Sunset Island, who haunt the riven decks
of Sweet Nagia. Grant me now this boon,
stranger of this strangest land,
stranger of a friendly hand,
give to me one ship and full crew, a crew
strong of arm and good of aim, stalwart
in the face of death, for of death we shall
see surfeit, of death we shall see plenty.
Arm we now with strength and valor,
though honor is a trinket no worthy
pirate needs. Arm we now!
Arm we now as soldiers

with Vadian ballistae, harpoon bows
and the liquid fire of the Isles off Freet.
Arm we now with one accord: vengeance
'gainst those devils of the sky, those dragons
over Sunset Island. Hoist the sails!
Tack her west! We sail to slay, we sail to slay!
Hear you, oh dragons over Sunset Island,
hear you my proclaim! Vegeance, death upon
your heads, death upon your heads I avow,
and souls if souls you have!
And souls if souls you have!
My wrath redoubles now, this heinous tale
to recount. Never mercy shall know this
heart again, never measure grief but in
the blood of dragons! Stranger, heed me now:
these beasts must be devoured
these devils be consumed
by our enmity, for they the fiercer blow,
they the fiercest blow have struck. One only
of their kind was killed, was slain,
of their kind only one was slain
by my ill-fated mate, my crew, my hand.
So now all must die, even as my crew and I,
yes, now all must die even as my crew and I.
Even as my crew and I—died to dragons,
even as Sweet Nagia's crew was slain
in the sky of Sunset Island,
over Sunset Island.

Utopian Moon Waning

Waning moon in garden sinuous bright,
hear her haunting wail! her demon lover
calls no more. the brood conceived, passion cooled,
farewells in flights of swift notes, dulcimer
notes, that sing of futures past, a damsel
wholly enchanted, Celestine lover
gone to win fortune and fame abroad. Dream
the day again an errant knight rides in
on steed of oath to have and hold, but no!
not this kind of love in that sunny dome
that pleasure dome of touch and go, sinning
bright the night away beneath a silvery moon—
just a passing fancy in a pantomime
of love caught under fair stars in ripe time.

And yet memory plays across the eyes—
our flashing eyes, our groping hands,
our lusting hearts and open minds.

Fillmore Lewis

Azieran: Brotherhood of Rot

Christopher Heath

Dusk fell on the outskirts of Clairmont Forest as Baarinar and his men approached on horse, having ridden over tall swaying grasslands several days from Ara'sante, Velusia's capital. They numbered a score in all, outfitted city guardsmen with light chain, long swords, and steel batons. Their captain, Baarinar Vultin, was set apart in that he did not don standard-issue armor, but rather wore heavy, lobstered black plate-mail to suit the occasion at hand. Great sword strapped to his side, he surged forward carrying a baton. The helm tethered to his saddle was the colour of pitch with a grated visor, upon which was mounted a hawk with its great dark wings spread open as if in flight.

Most of the men had been drinking heavily, displaying utter lack of wisdom by indulging in such spirits, despite the nature of their journey. The youngest, a man of only sixteen winters, sported a split lip where Baarinar's temper had flared in response to an ill-mannered jest.

"Do you even think Lorrincross will show?" Dairmil questioned, sober-eyed and staring into the tree line.

"I'm counting on it, of course," answered Baarinar, the captain of the guard for Ara'sante's River Ward. He was a hard-edged man of stocky build, a squat, brutish face framed by a thick black beard and accentuated with heavy eyebrows, deep-set eyes, and black hair that blew in wild tangles when the wind kicked up. He grunted a laugh. "You have seen his scouts as easily as I. They've circled us far and wide, ensuring the challenge is no trap set by King Karguuhn. He will come.

"Gods! My blood boils with thoughts of battle. The increased bounty on that traitor's head will pay off my villa and buy a fine dancing girl outright."

"Provided you are the victor, sir." Dairmil raised both brows with a look of concern, giving his thin, studious face an added weight.

Baarinar's lips turned upward with a smirk. Had those words come from another of his company, a sound beating would have been in order. "And how is a man, saint or otherwise, going to defeat me with a broken sword?"

"Broken sword?" Dairmil responded, then continued with one of his customary informed diatribes. "The legendary and holy Arinsorn is more than just a sword, it is whispered to be the sister blade to Myhrdrivvian, to be reforged from flames fed by the willing yet unclean flesh of a hundred enemies of the sword's makers. And when that happens, Myhrdrivvian will reveal itself at last in the hands of a usurper, heralding a new age for broken Armencadia!"

"For all your witching words of fate and new ages and usurpers, it is still just a sword to me, Dairmil. And a broken one at that."

"So be it." His sergeant's mind wisely drifted to more practical rumors. "They say that St. Lorrincross Lazure makes his opponents beg for mercy at the point of a misercorde."

"To Shayde with his dagger! That dog will beg for mercy when I flay him alive and hang his hide out to dry. His head will be at the palace gates by week's end. Mark my words."

"And what makes you think he'll honour your challenge, and this meeting won't turn into a bloodbath? Certainly, he could overwhelm our small band if he wished."

"He is a knight, a saint, regardless of his current station as an outlaw. Men of honour have that trait ingrained in them, and turn not lightly from the path."

"Desperation forces the hand where it would not otherwise go."

"Mock me again and I'll have you quartered. Lorrincross will show, and I am certain he will fight with that broken sword. The peasants also say he will show mercy, if asked. You would do well to put more stock in the chatter of commoners than old fables. At any rate, I fully expect to win this duel, though I've nothing to lose."

"If the stories hold true."

"They shall hold. All the peasants in these parts say it is so, as do our spies—who have born firsthand witness. There is no reason to have any doubt."

"I've not seen nor heard from any of these men who have been shown mercy, though many have ridden out from Ara'sante to claim the ever increasing bounty." Dairmil's eyes smoldered with skepticism.

"Because they were unskilled in the art of fighting and were beaten down by a broken sword. Bah! They slunk off to the shadows in shame to lick their wounds, and who could blame them."

"Ah, I think I see your challenger in the wings."

From the woods emerged two score plus of men, not the rabble one would expect from a band of refugees, but well clothed fighters, armed to the teeth. At their head, upon a white stallion, a large knight dressed in fluted plate mail polished to mirror perfection, embossed with tangles of slender licking flames which snaked their way across the silver surface, enameled with burnt orange pigment. Upon his head, a helm of polished steel, decorated in the countenance of a gleaming, fanged metallic dragon, St. Lorrincross Lazure staring out from its maw. A white cape with thread-of-gold border and an electrum chased clasp of platinum accentuated his station as the leader of this band. A black sheath of leather could be seen beneath his parted cape, and the coils of a steely white serpent forming the crossguard and hilt.

"Lorrincross!" Baarinar immediately called out, wasting no time. "You're a traitor to good King Karguuhn and his entire Armencadian Empire. A bounty is on your vile head, and I mean to take it."

"So I've heard," the saint commented, as if the charges set against him were light as silk. "However, it's widely known that Karrguhn is a pretender to the crown, and there currently is no Armencadian Empire. Perhaps when the true king steps forward to reclaim his rightful place on Velusia's throne, the kingdoms that were once Armencadia will coalesce, and the empire will be once more."

"Blasphemy!" Baarinar spat, dismounting. Men on both sides brandished blades or leveled crossbows, but all respected the challenge. Only two men would fight this day.

"Then come collect your bounty," Lorrincross challenged, taking to foot in an instant, and drawing a broad sword from scabbard. It was immediately clear that the blade had been snapped in twain, and was now only two-feet in length, ending in a rough, jagged edge. The saint stuck the sword in the ground before him, and knelt in prayer, his lips whispering just above the pommel.

Baarinar placed helm upon head, then unsheathed his own blade, a capable wick of steel finely forged in Velusia's royal smithy and worth three month's wages to a commoner. It was a great sword, not the one he normally carried on watch, but a family heirloom passed down several generations. The birthright felt heavy and powerful in his hands, spurring him onward with fanatical confidence as he charged.

Lorrincross remained stooped, deep in prayer, paying his aggressor little heed until Baarinar was fully upon him. As the captain of the guard drew back and swept the blade in an overhand arc, sending it downward with utmost force, Lorrincross kissed the pommel and drew it from the ground in an instant. He slashed sideways with all his might, performing what seemed near impossible—parrying the great sword with the broken blade and spinning his assailant in the process. The saint's other hand produced a shorter blade, its hilt merely a tangle of leather wraps and absent of cross-guard. It flicked forward in a blur, slashing the tendons just above Baarinar's heel, hobbling him in the process.

The saint quickly retreated, his misercorde dripping blood. Baarinar saw his opponent smiling through the great steel dragon's maw. The thin, fair face of Lorrincross seemed majestic and pure, bordering on divine . . . not at all what the captain had imagined of a traitor. The saint was tall and lean, though swift-footed, and circled his lame opponent with a grace that belied his stature. The men were silent. Breath shown as barely noticeable ghosts beneath a deep blue sky, which ever blackened as the sun dipped low, emitting its final rays while storm clouds rolled overhead. Baarinar struggled to turn with Lazure's movements, to remain facing his opponent. The saint no longer seemed like prey, as he had kneeling before the ground and whispering to invisible gods to aid his ruined blade. Now he was a cunning harbinger of death, a messenger whose purport was wrought in quick, slender steel.

"Come at me then, bastard!" Baarinar exclaimed, grimacing in pain. "I'll finish you yet." He held his weapon with both hands, positioned for a quick thrust. Darkness fell.

Lorrincross charged as Baarinar steadied himself, ready to lunge. The saint veered wide at the last moment, and the captain overextended. He connected with the great sword's point, but the blade was carried with momentum rather than strength, and thus deflected by armor. Baarinar lost his balance and fell, his great helm smashing into the ground, clumps of grass and dirt caught in his visor, blinding him.

The captain moved to loosen the helm as he arose, but then felt a foot on the small of his back, pushing him forward, down again. Pain shot through his right arm as a foot secured it to the ground. Agony coursed through his body at the loss of extremities by the cut of steel, and he instantly knew that he no longer clutched his birthright.

Baarinar, flung onto his back by strong, capable hands, felt the weight of Lorrincross was upon him, pinning him down. His helm was ripped from his head, and the large Azier moon shone down, reflected in the misercorde. Tatters of leather which formed its hilt brushed across his face as added insult. Lorrincross brought the blade lower, and placed the edge against Baarinar's neck.

"Mercy!" the captain shouted, keeping his wits about him despite the pain, anger, frustration, humiliation, and a thousand other emotions which cascaded and collided through his soul.

"Mercy?" Lorrincross responded, as if the word was foreign to him. "I could let you live . . . but my brand of mercy comes not without its price. You must kiss this blade I have at your neck, kiss it and swear fealty, flesh and mind, to the true emperor of Armencadia. Denounce Karguuhn, the Pretender King!"

"Yes! Anything. I will do it!"

The saint moved the blade from Baarinar's throat and placed it against his lips. The captain kissed it all too hastily and spoke the required oath, almost a whisper so that his men could not discern the vile words. But surely they had overheard his victor, surely he was ruined.

"I have waited long for you," the saint spoke cryptically. "We will meet again . . . we will meet again soon." Lazure arose and swiftly left the field of battle, he and his men fading into the woods, beneath the veil of night.

Baarinar struggled to his feet, noting his great sword and helm were missing from the field. Lorrincross. The saint had ruined him utterly — ruined him with a broken sword and a misericorde — he, the brutish guard who had quickly arisen through Ara'sante's ranks and gained a reputation for unmatched competence and cruelty. The captain struggled to his feet, watching as his men turned their horses to ride.

"Will none of you help me?" Baarinar spat, swearing aloud. "A field dressing before I bleed to death?" The captain held on high a hand covered in blood; only an index finger and thumb remained. He swooned at the sight as he shed his gauntlet, feeling lightheaded at the loss of blood, but no others offered aid.

He stepped forward, stumbling on his lame heel, falling to the ground and driving his bloodied hand in the dirt. Pain shot through his leg and arm, up his body, pounding his head. The captain reeled, then caught sight of two separate sets of hooves before him. He looked up.

Dairmil sat atop his roan mount, holding the reins of Baarinar's black stallion. He stared down, his expression caught between that of disappointment and satisfaction. "I warned you, Baarinar. Despite your successes, you have always discounted the advice of others, to listen to your own misguided braying. Don't look so shocked. The men heard the oath you took, so I would stay well clear of them, and well clear of Ara'sante. Ride where you will, but not with us. Lorrincross killed Baarinar, Captain of the River Ward. Now you are Baarinar the Homeless, Baarinar Without a King. I am done with you." Dairmil spat upon the ground, letting fall the reins of his former captain's stallion. He dug his heels into the sides of his horse and galloped off.

Baarinar struggled to his feet, reaching for his saddlebags. He procured a wineskin, taking a draught before dousing the rest on his wounds. His eyes watered from the pain as he grunted in agony. Locating a change of clothes, he ripped the tunic and wrapped a strip tight around his ankle. His hand was dressed as well, a strip held in place with his other hand while the knot was pulled tight with clenched teeth and a jerk of the head. The deposed captain screamed in anguish when it was over.

He sucked wind, steadied himself, and mounted the steed by putting his unharmed foot in the stirrup and swinging himself over. Baarinar swore aloud as the other foot crashed against the mount, and his pain redoubled. With a one-handed flick of the reins he was off, heading east for no particular reason. He knew Ara'sante was to the southeast, but he would stay well north. Vast Permencian Lake lay fifteen miles away, and that would mean fresh water, fishermen, and trappers. He had fifteen shines of silver and a gold to his name, enough to keep him comfortable for awhile.

Baarinar looked at his hand. He wanted to curse the saint, but was too preoccupied thinking of his future—there were no more comforts of city life and a good wage to be had. He must forge ahead again, now lame. Azieran was not the world for a cripple; fortunes were built on stout backs, superior swordsmanship, or crafty scheming. None of these suited him now.

He rode slowly, feeling weak, and only after five miles had been covered he settled down for the night beneath a small lean-to assembled with much difficulty, and then crawled into his bedroll. The cold was tearing at his fortitude and the winds would certainly extinguish any attempt at building a fire. Then the rains came crashing down amid strokes of lightning. He shivered most of the night and awoke in the early morn all the worse for wear. At least the deluge had subsided to mere drizzle.

He arose with sore muscles and aching wounds. Examining the bandage on his hand—stained crimson black and still seeping—he grimaced at this misfortune, as if a night's poor rest could have driven it away, made it all just a dream. His ankle was cut deep, and that, too, was a nagging misery. "I should have asked Dairmil for more spirits," he muttered to himself, longing for the pain to ease.

Baarinar struggled to load his horse and then mount it, eager to be on his way and find shelter near the lake. He rode across a gently rolling plain frequented by small copses of trees, but met no travelers on the wide expanse. It was by chance that he glanced down to find a mysterious, raised copper-coloured patch upon the index finger of his wounded hand. He touched it with his other hand, but mysteriously felt no sensation. Puzzled and worried, he had no choice but to push it from his mind. After several hours of riding, at last the shores of a vast, crystal blue lake were spotted. The sun was shining bright, warming the late morning air.

A small, solitary hillock among the trees arose to the north, from which smoke appeared. And as it drew Baarinar's gaze, it also drew his curiosity. The ruined, former captain directed his horse in that direction.

As the trees began to form a dense canopy overhead, a footpath was found, appearing to lead toward the hill. Baarinar spurred his horse in that direction, entering a deep wood of still and eerie silence. After winding around several small mounds, he approached the high, craggy hillock, noting a triptych of large stone slabs forming an archway on high. Smoke rolled from natural vents near the top of the stony rise.

A figure swathed from head to toe in tattered robes appeared to greet him. "Greetings," the mysterious stranger hailed in an amiable, excited voice. "At last you've come."

"Who are you?" Baarinar Vultin demanded.

"Your brother. Come. Come. The others await!"

"Bah! What madness is this? I'm not your brother, stranger."

The man paid no heed, motioning the wounded traveler to follow him into the hill. He quickly disappeared.

Baarinar nearly turned his steed around to ride off, but something—curiosity or hunger perhaps—compelled him to dismount and climb the path, to journey where the entrance awaited ominously halfway up the steep mound. The path to the cave was well-worn, though the defeated captain favored his healthy foot as he struggled in pain. A dry heat escaped the gaping entrance beneath the massive triptychs, and the interior glowed sporadically with the flicker of flames.

As he entered, the cave seemed foreboding to his eyes, and the wind whistled as a siren's song, bringing a foetid stench of decay which caused him to recoil. Bronze sconces adorned the walls at constant intervals, and the light shed by torches made them seem as bastions harkening to a path of forlorn mystery. The tunnel curved in an ever tightening downward spiral with no side passages to be found. His senses told him that he had ventured near ground level, or perhaps below, and he continued along in hurried, limping flight despite his aching ankle. He now heard many strange mutterings mixed with the chirpings of bats, as if a reticent convocation progressed in the depths below.

The hair on Baarinar's neck prickled, and so he halted, nearly turned and ran as any sane man might have done. But having journeyed thus far, he felt obligated to at least glimpse the events transpiring below. The stench of decay intensified. He rounded a bend to discover a bright orange glow as the sounds grew louder.

His feet carried him abruptly and suddenly into a vast, dank underground chamber of stalactites, where scores of men in filth and tattered robes knelt in prayer before a great forge scripted in platinum runes, majestic fires beneath the great polished iron furnace flaring like angry efreets. The flames arose up through a hole at the forge's apex where a metal slab was affixed. A sense of awe washed over Baarinar as he regarded the furnace and in a supernatural daze stumbled further into the chamber, throngs of madmen groping at him in what seemed a display of religious fervor. He pressed on through the masses, till a figure stopped him cold — the man he met at the hillock's entrance.

"What is this place?" Baarinar questioned, his tone now subdued and meek for the first time since his youth.

"It is where we belong," the voice answered.

"I don't understand."

"Tavvinok explains it best. He's the one that discovered the secret and meaning of our existence, where once we were lost."

"Then you should take me to him," Baarinar responded, in a near catatonic state, having been overwhelmed by the sights and sounds transpiring. The name of Tavvinok sounded vaguely familiar.

The figure nodded and led him to the front of the throng, next to the gaping furnace, where a hulking figure in tattered robes sat on a throne of decaying wood, bored through with a thousand tiny holes wrought by insects and worms.

"At last you've come," the figure spoke, in a deep, booming voice.

"Who are you? What place is this?" the exiled captain questioned, too overwhelmed for his voice to inflect any annoyance.

"I am Tavvinok of Ara'sante." The large figure stood and let fall his tattered robe, revealing a body covered in raised, copper-colored lesions. Baarinar remembered his distinct, angular face. He was a famed gladiator, who left Ara'sante years ago with the promise to return St. Lorrincross Lazure to justice.

"What are you doing here?" Baarinar gasped.

Swift as the strike of a snake Tavvinok lashed out with mighty arms, grabbing his weakened inquisitor by the neck and forcing his head next to the gleaming iron surface of the forge. "Look, you fool! What do you see?"

Baarinar would have recoiled in horror had not Tavvinok's mighty thews held him in place. The terror wrought by great splotches of raised, rust-colored patches covering his face caused him to cry out. "What has become of me?"

"You are a leper," the gladiator spoke, his words inflected with a sense of finality. "As are all in this colony."

"How did this happen?" Baarinar's legs felt weak, his mind reeled.

"That is what all ask who come here," Tavvinok returned. "How does one contract the advanced stages of leprosy overnight, and feel compelled to live in this colony, unable to escape though no doors or locks bar the way?"

Baarinar regarded him with tearful eyes, awaiting an answer to make some sense of this nightmare dread.

"Lorrincross. Each of us here has faced him; each of us has been defeated. You knelt and kissed the misercorde? You swore the oath, did you not?"

Baarinar nodded, feeling sick in his stomach.

"You fool. We are all fools. That was no simple misercorde or unbinding oath which we greedily spat in hopes of mercy." The words which followed stunned Baarinar as he had never thought possible, and drowned his soul in pure, unadulterated woe. "You swore an oath on the broken blade of Arinsorn, kissing the legendary sister blade of Myhrdrivvian without even realizing it!" Tavvinok recanted the oath. "I swear fealty, flesh and mind, to the true emperor of Armencadia. I denounce Karguuhn, the Pretender King."

And so, too, the words of Dairmil came to Baarinar's mind. *Arinsorn is whispered to be the sister blade to Myhrdrivvian, to be reforged from flames fed by the willing yet unclean flesh of a hundred enemies of the sword's makers. And when that happens, Myhrdrivvian will reveal itself at last in the hands of a usurper, heralding a new age for broken Armencadia!*

"What is to become of me?" Baarinar asked, not yet fully comprehending his fate.

"We are now exactly a hundred in number," the gladiator responded, coldly. "Now we will pay our due. The mercy of Lorrincross comes not without a price."

The masses suddenly became somber and silent, filing uniformly before the great open forge. Baarinar stared upward, shocked to see St. Lorrincross Lazure in his shining armour standing atop the furnace and seeming divine, the two halves of Arinsorn in his hand. He had kept his promise they would meet again soon. The saint unwrapped the makeshift hilt of leather wraps from the shorter blade—what was once thought of as a misercorde—and then placed both halves on the metal slab, their broken ends touching. They would be reforged by ensorcelled flames fueled by the flesh of his defeated enemies.

"Come," Tavvinok bade. "Let us take our places in line. Our rotting flesh must be cleansed by the flames; we must pay our price."

Baarinar nodded. There was no longer hatred in his soul for the mighty saint who bested him and ruined his life, only a sense of indebtedness. He felt compelled by his own sense of obligation.

One by one, a hundred lepers stoked the fires of destiny, reforging Arinsorn and setting into motion events which would herald a new age at the behest of Myhrdrivvian, its sister blade. The Armencadian Empire would soon be united once again.

THE SUN OR THE MOON

Cheryl Peugh

Anala paused on the threshold and studied the room before her with a narrowed gaze. Shelves of folded fabric lined the walls. The cloth merchant, Doban, had already shown her the moth damage on several skeins of wool. She considered. The Right-Hand Path spells were those of revelation, of truth, of guidance. Since she wanted to know how the moths managed to get into the room, Sun magic seemed appropriate.

Picturing the spell she wanted in her mind, and what she needed it to accomplish, Anala built the power between the fingers of each hand as if she shaped an invisible sphere. The image of the sun on her forehead flared to brilliant life. She tossed the sphere into the air, and the spell unraveled and covered the room like a net.

"What's she doing?" Doban asked, restless.

"You asked us to find what brings the moths into your goods. She searches," Enera said.

"I'm paying good money for results, Sunmaster."

"And you'll get them, Merchant Doban. Please be patient."

Anala blocked out the intrusive voices and concentrated on what the spell told her.

A deep sparkle in one corner of the room caught her eye. She let her spell unwind and reveal the secret of the moths in the cloth goods. The blurry, indistinct image of someone stood in the corner and released sparks of light that flittered around the room. The image remained dark and shadowy, but the moths had no magic but that of their own lives, and the trails of light essence each and every one had left behind shone in Anala's eyes.

"Every few weeks, during the evening hours, moths are brought here and released in this corner. The person who brings them is disguised as someone you know," Anala said. "A tall lad with a scar on one cheek."

"Terzil," Doban said, disgusted. "I trusted him."

"Merchant Doban, did you not hear her?" Enera said. "Terzil did not do this. Someone disguised as Terzil releases the moths."

"I'll fire Terzil! When this person comes to release the moths, I'll have the constable waiting for him."

"Can you handle the shop on your own?"

"No. I would have to bring in another worker," Doban admitted.

"Whoever is doing this would adjust the spell to appear as your new worker," Enera pointed out.

He scowled. "How do I stop this?"

Enera looked at Anala. "Child?"

Anala considered the Left Hand Path. Its spells were those of concealment, of subterfuge, of misdirection. She felt the Sun sign on her forehead grow cold, and the Sun magic she had been using wavered and died. She felt the slightest twinge of sadness at the demise of the warmly brilliant spell, but she shrugged off the feeling.

The crescent moon on the left side of the sun on her forehead gleamed to life. Anala traced the outlines of the inside of the doorway with her finger. The cool blue gleam her finger left behind sank into the wood and disappeared. Anala looked at Enera.

"Moon magic. I have set a spell of misdirection on this doorway, Sunmaster. Once he enters, he shouldn't be able to find his way out again. The spell will trigger at nightfall and will hold until light penetrates the room."

"A simple and elegant solution, child. Merchant Doban, I suggest you rise with the dawn every day until you have caught the perpetrator."

"You may be sure that I will," Doban said grimly. "I will send the agreed upon silks to the school as soon as I can gather the requested amount. I thank you, Sunmaster. This means much to my business and my reputation."

"Do not thank me, Merchant Doban. Thank the Undecided," Enera said.

Doban gave Anala a stiff nod. She gave an inner sigh, knowing what he thought, what most Varchenians thought, of the Undecided. The Sungod Zi featured large in the lives of Varchenians, and the Emperor held to an official stance of sun worship. Sunmasters were favored. Varchenia discouraged

Moonmasters from living anywhere within its borders. The only Moonmasters Anala knew dwelled within the walls of her school. Oh, not that Moon magic wasn't practiced in Varchenia—but not openly. Varchenians tolerated the Undecided up to the point of Decision because they were useful, and some would eventually become Sunmasters.

Anala followed Enera from Doban's shop. The noise and bustle of the crowded street outside hit her in the face like a slap, and the heat of the afternoon sun pressed down on her. People parted in a wave before the Sunmaster's progress, and Anala walked in the lee of the woman's wake, a smaller vessel behind a greater ship.

The rich red and gold of the Sunmaster's headdress belonged in this city of thick stone and deep earth, Anala thought. Not like the cool greens and blues of the country farm where she had spent the first ten years of her life. Anala realized she hadn't thought of home for a long time. Five years. A sudden longing to walk the green hills of her father's farm rose in her. Maybe she could figure out which Path she wanted to take while walking among the flowering meadows and whispering trees, and listening to the wisdom of her parents. She would turn fifteen this summer, and that made her one of the oldest Undecided at the school. Others who had started with her had already Decided.

Eventually, they turned onto narrower, less crowded, streets, and Anala walked at her teacher's side.

"Sunmaster, has anyone ever not Decided?" she asked in a brooding tone.

Enera turned to look at Anala with bright blue eyes. "Orlen," she said. "And even he Decided at the end of his life; he chose the Right-Hand Path."

"Did he live long?" Anala asked, interested.

"No," Enera said, blue eyes sad. "Orlen lived his twenty years with the mind of a very young child. A horse kicked him in the head early in his childhood. Quite a waste of talent—he would have been a strong Sunmaster had his mind been right."

The two walked in silence while Anala thought.

"I don't really want to Decide, Sunmaster. I like being able to draw on both Paths."

Enera smiled at her. "Of course you do," she told Anala. "That is because your point of Decision has not yet happened. Once you reach that place, you will know which Path it is that you are destined to take. That Path will become yours, and you will not wish to follow or draw upon the other Path. Once you Decide, all your power will be directed into one path and you will reach your fullness of strength. We all have to Decide sooner or later. You will choose — the Sun or the Moon. That's the way it's always been."

They had reached the gates of the school. Thick walls surrounded the great structure. Anala thought of the echoing, cavernous rooms and wandering hallways that had become her second home. Leaving it would be a wrench. If — when — she Decided, she would be expected to utilize her talent to support herself in whatever Path she chose.

Just inside the gate, Enera went on to her quarters, and Anala walked to her next class in a leisurely manner.

She paused in front of the door of an occupied classroom. The intent attitude of a circle of students caught her attention, and the tickle from her Moon sign heralded the presence of Moon magic. Inside the circle, she saw that one of the Moonmasters had two students giving a demonstration of binding magic. Anala recognized the Moonmaster. Cobor, dour and stern, who taught fourth level Moon magic since Stilin died last spring of a lingering illness.

He had two of the fourth level Undecided facing each other, Tania and Horic. Anala frowned. She thought that an uneven match. Horic, thin and dreamy, tended to avoid confrontations. Tania sought them out. She had an amazing talent for spells of offense and knew it. Anala found her sullen and abrasive, but their paths did not often cross.

"In any magical confrontation, you must focus on the spells you will use for defense and offense," he said. "You must hold both in your mind and let nothing distract you. Now let's see what you've got."

Tania called up a sphere of power that she tossed at Horic before he could ready his spell. The sphere unwound around him in an almost lazy manner and enclosed Horic in shadowy ropes, binding his hands to his sides. Horic fell over and looked up at her helplessly.

Anala's frown deepened as she saw that Tania did not release Horic once she had demonstrated the binding spell. Her hand crooked and the bonds around Horic tightened. He gave a grunt of fear and struggled against the spell.

"I don't think that's fair, Tania," another student said. "At least give him a chance to defend himself." Anala identified him as Rasy.

Cobor waved at him, concentrating on Tania. Anala didn't like the avid look in his eyes, or the intent, set look in Tania's. "Mercy is a weakness you can't afford," he said to her in a low voice. "Do what is necessary to win."

Horic squeaked as the bonds tightened again, his mouth opening and closing, trying to draw enough air to breathe. His lips had a tinge of blue.

Anala called up a simple spell of light and tossed it into the room between Tania and Horic. The spell exploded with a blast of light that rocked everyone back on their heels. Tania screamed and threw her hands in front of her face. The bonds around Horic disappeared and he drew in a whooping breath.

Cobor turned, mouth snarling, eyes tearing, and blinked at Anala standing in the doorway.

"What do you think you're doing, girl?" he said. "How dare you interfere!"

"He couldn't breathe! Couldn't you see that?"

"He needs to learn to defend himself," Cobor said tersely.

Anala stared at him. "How is letting Tania squeeze the life out of him teaching him to defend himself?"

"It wasn't fair!" Rasy interjected.

"Do you think an enemy is going to give him a chance?" Cobor shouted. "Do you think an attacker would stop just because he's on the floor? Life isn't fair! It's time you all knew that!"

The students stared, not used to seeing a teacher shout.

"I don't think the Superiors would consider suffocating Horic to prove your point the right thing to do," Anala said.

Mention of the Superiors brought Cobor up short. She watched him control his anger. He glanced at Horic. Rasy helped him stand as he shook and shuddered, drawing in great gasps of air. Tears from the light spell and from fright ran down Horic's thin face.

"He'll be all right," Cobor said.

Anala turned to leave. Rushing footsteps and the tingle in her Moon sign gave her a moment's warning. She whirled, the spell already leaving her hands. Tania's binding spell met the edge of Anala's shield wall and bounced off harmlessly.

"I challenge you to a duel, Anala!" Tania said in a high voice. "A duel of arcanum!"

Anala gave her a look of disgust. Tania's eyes were bloodshot and tearing, but the fury in them burned high.

"I'm fifth level, you're fourth. That would be about as well-matched as you and Horic."

"I gave you a challenge, clodfoot!"

The other students gasped. Anala narrowed her eyes at the insult to her country upbringing.

"Have a care, Tania," she growled.

"Challenge is given and witnessed," Cobor said in a smooth voice. "Do you accept?"

Anala looked at him. He could keep his face immobile but his eyes gave him away.

"Don't do it, Anala," Rasy said suddenly. "He—"

Rasy snapped his mouth shut under Cobor's glare.

"I challenge!" Tania shouted.

Anala looked at her, then Cobor, and her mouth tightened. She'd fallen neatly into their little trap. They'd been looking for someone to challenge worthy of Tania's skills, and she'd given them the excuse they needed. Well, maybe Tania deserved a taste of her own medicine.

"Fine!" Anala snapped. "Challenge accepted."

Tania smirked. A flare of satisfaction lit Cobor's eyes.

"As the one being challenged, I choose the time and place," Anala continued. "Dawn, at the Pit."

Tania lost some of her smirk. "Dawn! Couldn't you choose a decent—"

"Those are the terms," Anala said. "Take them or leave them."

She turned and stalked away, angry with Cobor, angry with Tania, and angry with herself.

† † †

"Are you out of your mind!" Enera said. "Duels are frowned on by the Superiors, you know that."

"She challenged me," Anala said, "and she half-killed Horic. I'm sure Rasic told you about the duel. If he did, he surely told you how it happened. I had no choice."

"There are always choices, Anala."

"Will you tell the Superiors?"

Enera had found Anala in her quarters, meditating in preparation for tomorrow's duel. The Sunmaster paced the center of Anala's small room. She didn't answer the question directly.

"Did you ever wonder why certain personalities seem to be attracted to Moon magic, and others to Sun magic, child?"

Anala shook her head, wondering what Enera hoped to accomplish. The challenge had been given and accepted. She couldn't withdraw now.

"The Left Hand Path attracts the secretive, arrogant, less empathic of us—those who like illusion and cold power for power's sake."

Anala stared at her teacher from underneath her brows. "Are you saying that the Left Hand Path is evil? I can't believe that. Moonmaster Diavar is not evil. I don't feel evil when I use Moon magic."

"No, child, the Left Hand Path is not inherently evil, nor are the people who use it. What I'm telling you is that it attracts the dark among us. I have heard—rumors—about Cobor and Tania. I do not trust either one of them. I fear for you."

Enera reached into the pocket of her robe and pulled out something she cradled in her hands. Her blue eyes reflected uncertainty, uncharacteristic for her.

"I have come to look upon you as a daughter, Anala. I wish to give you this."

Anala reached out her hand and accepted what Enera handed her. She looked at a sphere of crystal. Embedded inside the crystal were the dual signs of the Undecided. The sliver of moon gleamed with a pale light, nearly eclipsed by the warm amber glow of the sun.

"It's beautiful," Anala said.

"Teliac shaped this crystal when he was Undecided."

"Teliac?" Anala said, astonishment in her face. "But he Decided when he was ten years old! That would mean he shaped this—"

"When he was nine years old. Yes. Teliac had many talents besides being the greatest Sunmaster that Varchena has ever seen."

"You're giving this to me?" Anala asked in wonder.

"I am. Teliac made it to help him focus his magic. It has lain in the artifact room for a good number of years. As you can see, a residue of magic remains in the crystal. It should help you tomorrow."

Anala stared deep into the crystal and saw the slumbering magic needing only the slightest touch to awaken. . . .

When she looked up, Enera had gone.

† † †

The Pit lay in deep shadow, early morning sunlight not yet reaching an angle to shine inside it.

Anala paused. People waited on the edge of the Pit, backlit by the light of the rising sun. The story of the duel had spread. She spotted Enera and a few other Sunmasters. Cobor watched as well, standing at a distance from the knot of Sunmasters. Undecided lined the Pit.

She brought her eyes back into the Pit to let them adjust to the dimmer light.

In the past, the Pit had been dug to contain magical duels, both Undecided and Master alike. Earlier eras had been more ready to duel, evidently. The earthen walls of the Pit had been spelled to contain and nullify any stray magic that might escape.

Anala saw Tania approach across the stamped-earth floor and stop a few feet away, facing her. Anala gave her a bow. Tania responded with a slight inclination of her head.

Anala reached in her pocket to give the crystal sphere a reassuring touch, just as sunlight touched the rim of the Pit. A jolt of magic from the crystal transfixed her. Her awareness seemed to expand—to grow larger than the Pit, to grow as large as the city—and she knew what awaited Merchant Doban in the cloth room of his shop.

No! She breathed out the denial in her mind, unable to scream out the word.

She came to herself and gasped out, "Tania! We must stop! There's a kobol in Merchant Doban's shop. He must be warned!"

Tania gave her a slow smile. "When I am through with you, the constable will come arrest you for the murder of the cloth merchant. I will pretend to be as shocked as the rest of the school that a fifth level could be so negligent, so sloppy in her magic as to trap a kobol where it could harm the non-magical."

The Moon sign on Anala's forehead hurt so much she could barely speak through the pain. "But why?"

"Because you made a fool of me, that's why!" Tania said through her teeth. "And you diminished me in his eyes! For that, you're going to pay."

Stunned and horrified, Anala jerked her gaze from Tania to Cobor and back again. She suddenly realized what kind of rumors Enera had been hearing.

"How did you know about the spell I set?" Anala asked. "That was not common knowledge."

"My dear Anala, who did you think the other cloth merchants would hire to release the moths in Merchant Doban's cloth room? A trickster off the street? They came to the school, dolt! Moonmaster Cobor took their money and entrusted me to do the magic."

Anala looked up and locked eyes with Cobor. By some trick of the sun, he stood out clearly. The satisfaction on his face gave her all the answer she needed.

"He said I'm going to be the best that ever was. Better than Stilin. Better than him, even. Far better than a clodfoot like you! I'm going to be the greatest Moonmaster since the rise of Fancor."

Anala winced at the mention of Fancor's notorious name—a name written into history with blood and terror. She looked at Tania and noticed for the first time that only the Moon sign shone on her challenger's forehead and grew cold to the tips of her fingers.

"You've Decided," she whispered.

Tania's smile widened, and Anala noted the black sphere of power growing between her fingers. She only had time to close her hand about the crystal again before the spell of pain hit her.

Waves of agony locked her muscles. Her hand gave a spasm but retained the crystal.

Her mind remained clear under the pain. She realized that Enera had been right. There were always choices. She could choose to remain Undecided, and perhaps win this duel even yet, letting Merchant Doban pay the price for her staying Undecided a few more days or weeks—or she could Decide now, and forfeit the duel, saving Merchant Doban's life. Maybe it wasn't a choice after all.

Pain itself was a form of power. A small amount of pain refined and focused the faculties. Agonizing pain sometimes gave strength beyond normal limits. Anala opened herself up to the pain that seared her body. She tapped its energy, the energy she felt in the crystal, the energy she soaked up from the sun, and reached out to Merchant Doban's shop. The nullifying spells in the walls of the Pit hindered her until her combined energies overcame their influence.

The rage of the kobol struck at her senses. It wanted to hurt, to rend, to kill. It especially wanted to hurt the one who had summoned it.

She could dismiss the kobol to the Underworld even from this distance, but if Anala could bring the kobol to Tania, the creature would expose her as its summoner to the watching people.

The kobol appeared in the Pit between Tania and Anala. The scaly, horned, and tailed creature of the Underworld bellowed out its challenge to Tania.

Tania gasped in fear, and the pain in Anala's body abruptly ceased.

Now here was evil in all its ugliness, Anala thought hazily as the creature bellowed again. Ridges of bone down its upper arms and on its tail made it formidable. As if the six-inch claws weren't impressive enough.

The creature's red eyes fixed on Tania. Her courage broke and she ran, but fell before she could reach the stairs. The kobol snaked after her, snarling.

Anala could hear the shouts and screams from the rim of the Pit, but no one could help them. The walls of the Pit stopped the spells each one tried to make, and none had time to combine efforts.

She deserves everything she gets, a tiny part of Anala said. She frowned. That sounded too much like someone else.

Mercy is a weakness you can't afford. Anala heard Cobor's voice in her mind. She knew that wasn't true. Mercy separated man from beast. Her parents had demonstrated that every day through decisions made on the farm for the benefit of both people and animals under their care. That firm standard had been instilled in her for the first ten years of her life, and five years away from her parents had done little to shake their influence.

She raised the crystal sphere above her head. Anala felt the sun blaze through the crystal and burn through her mind. Golden light streamed from between her fingers and washed over the kobol.

The creature screamed in high-pitched agony, twisting and turning, but the beam of light followed. The kobol faded away, banished back to the Underworld. The beam of light continued until it bathed Tania in its glow. Tania threw up her hands to protect her eyes and screamed like a madwoman, trying to roll away from the light and the eyes of everyone watching.

At the rim of the Pit, Anala saw Cobor turn and walk away. Later, she promised him in her mind.

Anala sighed, dropping her hands. The Sun sign on her forehead felt warm and comforting. She stared up at Enera.

The Sunmaster looked both stunned and pleased. You've Decided, she mouthed.

"Everyone Decides sooner of later," Anala whispered. "The Sun or the Moon. That's the way it's always been."

CHANGELING

Edward J. McFadden III

There are few fears that invoke uncontrollable horror or savage rage, yet the bond between a mother and child can bring out these feelings in a woman, cause her to lose touch with reality and act out of malevolence rather than rationality. The loss of a child can leave scars that never heal; memories that linger long after all the relevant facts are forgotten. The Elves empathized with these feelings, but their plight went beyond the loss of a few human children.

Long ago the Elves faded from the world as we know it, leaving no trace that they had ever existed, no mark to reveal their majesty and grace. Fleeing far away, concealing themselves within the mists, the Elves kept an endless vigil. Praying and hoping that the sickness that had befallen them would ease so they could return to the world of the living, but prayer and wishes yielded naught but anguish. All children born to elvin parents were peevish and sickly. Many died shortly after birth and those who lived became shadows, never speaking or contributing to the lives around them, slowly fading and becoming as dead things, mere shells of life.

The lineage of the Elves was failing.

It was Bergan, the king's son, who had first conceived the idea of the Changeling, a hope that could restore the elves. "Father, mankind has so many healthy children—could we not take just a few and leave our sickly newborns behind?" asked Bergan.

"Nay, my son. You think only of the elves, as is your wont, but I am King and I cannot forsake other life for the saving of our own."

"But you ere, my lord. We would not forsake life! The children would be happy here and in time their parents would have more children and most likely forget!"

"Nay! They would never forget."

As their plight became more grievous, many of the elves began to whisper of the Changeling, questioning the king's decision not to allow Bergan to try his plan. Many believed that humans were the root cause of their plight, and didn't understand why the king was letting their children die, or worse, become shadows. Human's had polluted, destroyed, and abused the earth, and these wounds, some believed, were why the elves were dying.

As the years wore on and less and less elvin children survived, the king was forced to consider Bergan's plan, and after much debate, feeling he had no choice, let Bergan attempt his plan.

"My dear Elves, it has been decreed that I and one other shall journey through the mists of fairy back to the world of men and thereby save our race from the plight that has befallen it. I ask now . . . I plead now, for one of you to give up that which is closest to you, to help me take the first step in restoring us to life," yelled Bergan as he stood before the last of the elves. All were silent, and looked upon Bergan with wonder, valor in their hearts and sorrow in their eyes.

Finally an old gray elf spoke. His long beard trailed to the floor and his pointed ears spiked outward through his long salt and pepper hair. His voice was thin and frail, yet it held a majesty that caught the attention of all present. "I have seen many ages of the elves, yet I see not what you speak of, my lord."

"I mean to do that which my father feared to do! I shall replace one of our sickly children, a Changeling, with a young healthy child. Who will give up their child?" Everyone stood as still as stone, waiting, breathing, hoping that the young prince's gaze would not fall upon them. "I ask again! Who will make the sacrifice?"

Bergan knew he was asking his follows to do that which he himself could not do. In his youth, when his father had begun to teach him what it meant to be king, he had told the young freckled Bergan that he should never ask another to do what he himself was unwilling to do. He scanned the crowd, reading the familiar faces for fear, doubt, anything that would indicate his volunteer.

Then something occurred to him: what if no elf came forward? How would he choose?

"We shall," said a young elf woman as she stepped forward with her child in hand and her husband in tow. The frail woman looked frightened beyond belief. Her eyes were wide with fear and uncertainty, and she was so white she looked to be almost albino. Her husband, a worn looking elf who himself didn't look very healthy, stepped at her heals, his gaze never leaving his newborn son.

The child was nothing but a ragged bag of creamy skin and feeble bones. His eyes were translucent, and he stared at the ceiling, not appearing to notice what was going on around him. The child gurgled, and drool tainted with blood seeped from the child's mouth.

Seeing this, the mother said, "I ask only one thing, my lord. How will one child help?"

"If I am successful we shall continue to replace our Changelings for hale children until we are restored."

"But my lord, if we mix our blood with that of lesser folk we will lose all that we have! Our magic will diminish and we shall become as men are, mortal," said the woman's husband.

"Yes, but 'tis better to live for what seems a short time, than to fester away like trapped animals," said Bergan. "It shall be done!" he continued as he stepped down from the dais and took the child from the sobbing woman.

The sun was just beginning to creep over the rim of the world, its orange brilliance burning away the haze, as prince Bergan, Restor, head of the palace guard, and the Changeling entered the mists of fairy. The young child cried as they walked, missing its mother and her familiar touch and caress. Restor stared at the young child, his heart feeling for him.

"My lord, 'tis what we do faithless? The Changeling is but a child, not capable of knowing what is happening," murmured Restor.

Bergan looked at Restor with a mix of pity and incomprehension on his face. Restor, all seven foot 380 pounds of him, looked like he would kill anyone or anything that got in his way, yet this tender question made the pit of Bergan's stomach feel as though a block of ice had taken up residence there. Trying to hide his frustration he answered, "The changeling will die. There is nothing we can do to stop that now. What we can do is help the children who are to come. Give them a chance at life." Restor did not answer.

Bergan stared forward into the mists, his mind swooning with self-doubt and fear. Then he spoke, "Sacrifice is sometimes faithless, my friend. I must try and see all ends." Bergan cradled the dying child in the crook of his left arm, his right hand firmly on the hilt of his sword.

The two elves walked on in silence, lost in thought. The mist became thicker, steady and unmoving before them. The air was still and cold. Bergan could feel a presence about them, an intelligence, and he felt like millions of ants were crawling across his brain. Abruptly, hundreds of small white dots of light became visible.

Once again the fairies had come to succor the elves.

Bergan and Restor paused and stared at the fairies. They floated like leaves on the wind of storm, their small padding wings shining in the translucent light that seemed to engulf them. Yellow light marked their keen eyes, and they seemed to disappear as they flitted within the mist.

"Hail those who helped us so long ago. Once again we ask thy help to . . ." but Bergan was cut off by a low murmur coming from the mists.

"Yes . . . it is those who helped you and we shall help again," said the fairies as the image of a nursery appeared.

A tall blonde haired woman stood next a crib looking down at a young infant. She held a bottle in one hand, her other caressed the baby's brow. She smiled so brightly upon looking at the infant that Restor's heart ached.

Bergan and Restor stared at each other, and Restor looked troubled, his elvin features haggard, eyes filled with doubt and apprehension. As Bergan gazed upon the nursery he too became uncertain. The mobile of blue and yellow unicorns which hung above the infant's crib twisted and spun, and the animals painted on the walls seemed to be alive and protective. "We have the right to preserve our race!" he shouted within his mind.

At that moment the woman looked up, staring around the room with a blank remorseful gaze as if she had felt some presence or some impending danger. She trembled for a moment, a chill racing up her back, the hair on the nape of her neck slick with sweat. Then unease passed, and she pulled the blanket over her baby and left the room.

Bergan and Restor stepped forward and looked upon the young child that would become the birth of the Elvin Nation. The child stared up at him with willing eyes as if he understood. As if he knew the immenseness of the moment.

Slowly Bergan reached down and picked the child up, and he laughed and giggled, looking at Bergan with a face painted of pure innocence. Bergan then turned to Restor and they exchanged the Changeling for the young human newborn. Bergan placed the Changeling in the crib and lifting his hands in a sign of superiority, cast the spell that he had so long waited and prepared for.

Before their eyes the Changeling seemed to transform, hiding its sickly face, becoming a parody of the human child. Immediately the Changeling appeared healthier, and his breathing became steady, his small fingers flexing with new found strength. This false hope only cast more guilt upon Bergan's breaking heart.

Restor looked on with wonder as Bergan left the crib and took the hope of the elves from his arms and cradled it in his own. "Yes, young Jimmy. You shall be the savior of my people," said Bergan, and as quickly as they had come, the two Elves and young Jimmy faded back into the world of fairy and were gone.

"Honey, did you hear that?" asked Jimmy's mother.

"No, I didn't hear anything," answered her husband.

"It came from Jimmy's room. I'm going to go check on him." Her husband only shook his head and wished that he got as much attention as his young son. She fussed over the child as if he were royalty: baby monitors, special laundry soap, clean clothes every few hours. He smiled, not wanting it any other way.

Slowly his smile faded as a nagging feeling of dread began to eat at him. Giving in to the feeling that something was indeed wrong, he got up and followed his wife.

With a shriek he darted into the infant's room and found his wife cradling their young son. She was weeping uncontrollably, yelling the child's name and screaming for God to bring him back. "Don't do this, please God — Please!"

Kneeling down next to his wife, Jimmy's father's worst fears were realized. The sickly Changeling had died. Jimmy's mother rocked back and forth, holding the dead infant in her arms, kissing his cold brow. His face had turned a light shade of blue, and the deep red of his thin lips had faded to nothing more then pale line with blood stained spittle dripping from it.

The police and ambulance arrived, but there was nothing that could be done. There was no apparent cause of death, no trace as to what had happened. After an extensive investigation and medical check, Jimmy's death was listed as just another crib death.

Though it may not have eased his mother's pain to know, Jimmy grew up to be an outstanding young man, marrying into a family of royalty and thereby helping restore the elvin people. As he grew, he himself helped contribute to what humans call crib death and what the elves call their only hope.

Dark Leviticus

Nathan Meyer

"Zach, I said no." Nora repeated.

"Come on, it's like being a member of the Mile High Club. You know, an *experience*." Zach argued.

"I have to finish this book, just knock it off."

"Ever since you started your feminist studies you've been a real joy."

"Is that what I am to you?"

"No, but having fun is part of being a couple."

"Is that the only kind of fun I can offer you? Is that all you see me as?"

"Never mind."

Defeated, Zach drove the SUV in silence for the next couple miles. Nora was immediately absorbed in her dog-eared copy of *The Da Vinnici Code*. The Everglades slid by as tall swamp grass reached up from still, black water. It had been twenty-two miles since the last town, a redneck enclave offering a taxidermist who advertised as 'specializing' in alligators and panthers. Both protected species as far as Zach knew.

His brother Jeff had recommended the route; he had taken it over Nora's protests. Jeff had heard from a guy who had a roommate whose cousin sometimes ran a package or two of coke up to Atlanta that this stretch of rural highway was never patrolled by State Troopers. It was true; he hadn't seen one since he'd turned off the turnpike and he'd kept the needle at over 80 mph pretty much the whole way.

Now the sun was getting low and the stretch of Everglades didn't seem to be ending. The road ran on an earth dike cutting straight across the swamp like a scar. The highway was dotted with road kill and the broken, pulpy bodies of opossums were strewn like punctuation marks along the double lane.

"Can I have a drink?" Zach asked.

Nora grunted a response and turned a page in her book. An accountant for NASA, Zach had first met her while working as a waiter at the Dixie Crossroads, in Titusville. Bent on proving to the world that she wasn't a boring number-cruncher or stereotypically straight-laced accountant, Nora had gone blonde, was addicted to the gym and had a great fondness for White Russians.

Two years in and her hair was mousy, she'd stopped drinking "because of the carbs" and had suddenly changed her Masters focus to feminist studies. Zach bitterly remembered coming home from shooting pool one night while Nora had been watching Jasmine, his seven-year old daughter from a high school girlfriend.

Daddy, are you Peter Pan? Jasmine asked.

No, why do you ask? Better than a six-pack down, he'd found the question cute.

'Cause Nora says you never grew up.

It had been a buzz killer.

"Nora, can I have a drink? From the cooler . . . please."

"Zach I think you've had enough beer; if you get pulled over, your server's license is going to get pulled."

"Anything you say, mom."

Bitch

Zach powered down the window and tossed out the empty bottle of Bud Light he'd been holding between his legs. He turned around and flipped the cooler lid open. He reached in, pushed Nora's Calorie One Pepsis to the side, found a Bud.

"*Zach!*"

He whipped back around just as the front of the SUV struck the little girl.

The wheel jerked hard in his hands and he stomped down on the brakes. The girl catapulted off her bike and tumbled through the air. She landed with a crunching *thump* on the hood of the SUV. She flipped up onto the windshield and, for a brief, eternal second, Zach looked straight into her face.

Her eyes were wide open as she screamed. She looked the same age as Jasmine. Blood splashed the windshield around her and then she was gone, snatched away by inertia. Zach heard her strike the roof once before he realized he'd cut the wheel too sharply. Nora screamed again and he twisted the power steering hard to keep it on the road. Over corrected. Now he was screaming.

The SUV's tires screeched in protest as the vehicle jerked sideways. Then the rubber caught on the pavement and Zach felt like he'd been teleported into a Tilt-a-Whirl. The roof caved in and then, just as suddenly, he was sitting upright again, looking out a windshield spider-webbed by cracks.

The Tilt-a-Whirl feeling snatched him again and they landed with a jar hard enough to rattle his teeth and cold, black water came rushing in through his open window. He hadn't bothered with wearing his seat belt and, in one surge of adrenaline, he pushed himself out of the open window.

He slogged around, confused for a moment, then got his feet under him. He pushed his Nikes hard against the muck beneath him and stood straight up. He broke the surface with a splash, gasping for breath. He cast wildly about for a panicked moment before realizing the water barely reached his waist.

He stopped his flailing, chest heaving. The SUV was upside down, cab under the filthy swamp water. The tires still turned and shock detached him, causing Zach to feel as if he were viewing the whole scene on a movie screen. The stagnant water stank, punctuated by the sharper chemical smell of gasoline.

Am I okay?

His hands flew to his body, felt his head. He was whole, saw no blood. He realized his shoulder was a little sore, and he was slightly dizzy, but other than that he didn't appear to have a scratch.

Thank God, Zach thought.

Then he remembered the little girl, panicked for a moment as he realized how much time he'd get for vehicular manslaughter. On top of that possession prosecution from two years ago, and there was no chance any bible-thumping central Florida circuit judge would let him walk with treatment and probation. Nora had to say she was driving, she hadn't touched a drop, her blood would be clean. Nora . . .

"Nora!" Zach yelled.

She wasn't coming out of her side of the SUV. Frantically he started to slog his way around the front of the vehicle. His foot twisted in the muck and he went down to one knee. He cried out in surprise and promptly gulped puissant water, soupy with organic clots. He came up to his feet with a sputtering cough.

Something snatched him by the back of the collar. His Old Navy t-shirt ripped as he was dragged down and he flopped into the water straight over onto his back. His arms were out in front of him, waving wildly. He caught a glimpse of the sun sinking beneath the waving grass before the water closed in over him like an executioner's hood.

He sensed swirling motion all around him, then felt hard blows punching through the water and striking him. A sharp, crushing force struck him in the stomach and he gasped reflexively. He sucked in a lungful of the dirty water and began panicking in earnest. It wasn't like in the stories; it wasn't easy, with a single blow striking him unconscious and letting him escape from the beating into blissful, dreamless sleep.

Zach was pummeled hard until he drowned.

† † †

The heat was stifling, pugnacious. Zach came awake to blinding pain. He tried to open his eyes and found he could only see out of his right one. He was half submerged in oily water but he could feel rough, broken cement beneath him. He groaned, a guttural sound, soft and low. The sound echoed back at him weirdly.

He rolled over and sat up. His head was on fire and, below that, he felt the surreal fuzziness he associated with really bad hangovers and concussions, both of which he'd suffered in abundance over the last decade or so. The left side of his face was sticky and tight with congealing blood. He reached a tentative hand up but jerked it quickly back, the slightest touch was excruciating. He'd felt a long flap of what could only be his scalp, dangling over the left side of his face in a curtain of bloody skin.

Feeling stupid and slow, Zach blinked and looked around him. Gradually images began to form out of the darkness around him. He looked up and saw night sky framed by broken walls of rubble that ran like a parapet around the massive hole he was at the bottom of.

It was obviously the cellar of a partially demolished building, a big one. Zach looked around again now that his vision had adjusted to the low light. The floor was covered with several inches of scummy, putrid water. The cellar was an upheaval of rubble piles and broken machinery in Jurassic proportions. It would make navigating through the mess as perilous as walking across the lava fields in Hawaii, where Nora had taken him on vacation six months ago.

Nora.

The girl and the crash and Nora trapped under the overturned SUV all came rushing back to him. Then the memory of being forced under water and the beating. Zach realized he had to get out of here. Someone had tried to kill him. They'd bashed his head with something and dumped him down here to hide the body. Even now, the would-be killer might be somewhere close by.

Zach felt his guts twist and writhe in surges of icy adrenaline. He leapt to his feet and almost fell down when his head exploded in fresh agony. He groaned down low in his throat and swooned. He cast about with his hand for support as brutal vertigo swept him. He felt waves of nausea crash against the beach of his stomach.

His hands came down on a protrusion of metal. He leaned into it and threw up. Each convulsion sent more lightening forks of agony through him. After awhile he stopped and the painful nausea receded. He wiped one hand against his mouth and looked at what he was leaning against.

It was a J-shaped erection of rollers between welded struts. In a burst of inspiration Zach realized what the building must be. It was a fruit packing shed. Oranges and maybe some other citrus—but surely oranges the most—had slid down out of the holding bins and onto conveyers just like this one. Conveyers manned by women with their hair held back by handkerchiefs, who smoked Marlboro lights on their breaks and bitched about how late the support checks were. Women just like

(my mom)

Zach had known growing up in the central Florida agriculture enclaves—women living in single wide trailers with daughters who were pretty easy to talk into bed. Daughters whose idea of making it better than their mothers was to get a job as cocktail servers in one of the big chain hotels around Orlando.

Sloshing through the water, Zach cast about him for some means of climbing up out of the cellar. It took awhile. He couldn't see very well in the low light and the edges of the industrial basement cast long, deep shadows. Reduced to the use of only one eye, he stumbled and tripped as he hunted through the ruin.

Eventually, he came to a set of wide cement stairs running straight up out of the pit. He hurried forward and, as he did, the shadows relented and he saw the yawning blackness of a doorway. Inside Zach caught a glimpse of narrow, crooked stairs running down into darkness.

He made a move toward the wide open stairs. As he did so a scrap of bobbing color caught his eye. Despite himself he stopped to look. It was the ripped-off cover of a paperback novel. The incongruity of this floating in the midst of all of the mechanical skeletons drew Zach's attention.

It was the paperback cover of *The Da Vinci Code*.

"So what," Zach said. He didn't realize he spoke out loud. "That thing sold about a billion copies. Could have been anyone's. Wind could have blown it down here."

He heard the startling echo of his own words and shut up in surprise. He turned towards the cement stairs. Something drew him up short and he took a hesitant step toward that black mouth of a doorway. Those stairs were wooden, looked potentially rotten. Anyone going down there

(into the dark, going down there into the dark, Zach)

would be taking their lives into their own hands. He didn't know, not really, that the cover was Nora's. Besides, even if it was, he needed to get help. Only a psycho would have taken advantage of someone in a wreck, who had just struck a little girl for God's sake, to kidnap and try to kill them. (The idea that it might have been from exactly just such a psycho that the little girl had been running didn't cross Zach's mind, not until much later.) He didn't have a chance against an armed, crazy killer in his current condition.

Hell, I'm lucky I'm not dead right now, he justified. In the back of Zach's mind the thought that it was okay because whoever had done this might be taking the time to rape or torture Nora, was there like the blackboard that the chalk of his thoughts was written on.

'. . . *you never grew up,*'

His shoulders slumped and he felt that uncomfortable twinge of shame. A shame at who he was. A shame that he'd been running from for quite awhile now.

He turned and walked through the doorway.

† † †

The doorframe over the top of the stairwell was buckled inwards, forcing him to duck under a beam to get onto the stairs. Cautiously, Zach approached the partially caved-in entrance. The idea that he could meet his attempted killer coming up as he was going down, was very prevalent in his mind. The caution saved his life.

He stepped up to the door and looked around the edges to see if anyone was hiding in the shadows. His eye flicked upwards in reflex at a dry whisper of motion. The snake was coiled around the broken splinter of door frame. If Zach had ducked under the beam to go through, he would have been shoving his face right into the hanging snake.

Zach almost tripped over his own legs in his hurry to scramble back. The snake was long and banded in stripes of yellow and red and black. He was forcibly reminded of the only good piece of advice Big Ed, one of his mom's numerous boyfriends, had given him.

Big Ed drove freight for Donald Duck orange juice. When he wasn't on the road he liked to watch the Marlins on TV and drink Budweiser. He'd point his finger like a gun at a teen-aged Zach and then belch like a sonic boom. He'd even taken Zach fishing on a couple of occasions, though Zach had really only gone along to keep his mother from bitching.

One day a coral snake had crawled around the cooler on the sluice bank and Zach had jumped out of his chair screaming. Big Ed belched. Then he'd reached over indifferently, with an oil stained boot, and toed the snake into the canal. He crumpled his beer can and whizzed it at Zach who was halfway to Ed's big Ford 350.

"Red and black never attack. Red and yellow kill a fellow," Ed quoted in his lazy drawl. He belched and reached for another beer. "You freakin idjit."

Now Zach was looking at another unexpected snake, and this one was, by God, red and *frickin'* yellow. A bite from a snake like that would damn well put a man *down,* and it would sure as hell kill him if he didn't get help but quick. No one could get past that.

Zach knew that was a lie. He was good at lying to himself, better even than he was at lying to others, and he was pretty much a past master of that little trick. He could pick up that length of metal pipe over there and beat the snake to a pulp. But the snake would be hanging above him and in order to hit it, he would have to get right underneath it and if he miscalculated it was *'red and yellow kill a fellow,'* as Big Ed had said.

Afraid to turn his back on the thing, Zach sidled over to the pipe. The snake watched him and as he approached it opened its mouth and hissed. It was coiled down in a sideways S shape, ready to strike.

If Zach missed he stood every chance of being struck. *This is stupid*, he thought. But the truth was that the next town was more than twenty miles back. If Nora had a chance, any chance, if there was even one to be had — then it was him.

Zach wasn't aware of his own sobbing as he moved towards the snake. All he was aware of was his fear. And, underneath the fear, the loathing he felt for himself for feeling it. He thought himself a whole lot better of a man than a Neanderthal like Big Ed, but the truth was, Ed would have grabbed that snake and bitten its head off. Then he would have marched down the rickety stairs and made whoever was down there pay dearly for the mistake of screwing with him in the first place.

Zach brought the pipe down and struck the snake in the head. The snake yielded before the force of his blow, knocked back. Zach jerked his arm out of harms way as the snake swung back towards him. But, it was already dead, its brains were pulped along the side of its head in jellied clumps.

Zach prodded the dead thing until it came loose and fell. He used the pipe to knock it out of his way. Then, checking doubly close, he carefully navigated the obstacle before the stairs. He was feeling pretty good about himself as he began making his way downwards.

† † †

In a darkness growing deeper with every step, Zach clung to the wall. Each step was a spongy, potential booby-trap under his feet. Below him he heard the constant *drip-drip* of seepage, repetitious as Chinese water torture. Several times he put his hands into cobwebs and hastily yanked them free. In Florida it wasn't only snakes that were poisonous.

Every couple steps he stopped and strained his ears in a vain attempt to catch the fleetest bit of sound. He strained even though he was more than half afraid that it would be Nora's screams he'd hear. For now, he only heard the cacophony of his beating heart.

About halfway down, Zach realized that throwing the pipe aside had been a stupid move. He thought about going back up to get it, but then admitted to himself that if he turned around now there is no way in hell he'd come back down. Cotton-mouthed with fear, he thought how good one of the Buds in the cooler would taste.

Near the bottom the black became so complete and threatening it seemed pregnant with insidiousness. He stopped to let his eyes adjust in the crypt-like darkness. It was dank at the foot of the stairs and he could tell by the earthy, moldy stench that it was below the cement foundations of the packing shed. *In* the ground now. Cellars aren't exactly common in Florida—the average water table was simply too high to make it plausible. The oddity of this cellar in the face of that engineering rule seemed more frightening to Zach than the dark.

He heard tiny claws scuttling. The sounds were small, however, and didn't cause him to panic outright. Instead, they added another layer of fear onto the coat Zach already wore. He used to shoot swamp rats with his pellet gun—up until Mrs. Kelly had made the class read George Orwell's *1984* in freshman

English. Since then, all he could think of when he heard rats was having his face stuck in a cage with one while it ate his eyes.

Zach stood up, uncomfortable at the thought of being so close to *their* level. He found he could see a vague irregularity in the darkness. A certain deep gray in the pitchblack that gave the suggestion of a door. He shuffled slowly towards it, mindful of tripping over something in the dark and sprawling out into some imagined pile of milling, savage rodents.

The closer he moved to the door the more readily he could make out the details of it. It scared him. Badly. It radiated a feeling of fearful unease the way an open freezer radiates cold. Zach didn't want to open that door. At the same time, as soon as he laid eyes on it he'd known, without question, that Nora was behind that door.

There was nothing modern about the door. It was set back in a natural alcove of earth, buttressed with an arch of rough stone. Into the arch strange markings had been carved. Zach would have called them hieroglyphics, only because he had no other word to describe them. They made no sense to him, but he knew they meant nothing good.

The door itself was made of iron with a heavy pull ring set at one edge. It was impossible to look at a structure of such heavy, simplistic design and not think about the door of a prison cell.

Portal, Zach thought suddenly.

That was what it was, not just a door, but a *portal.* He understood on some dim, reptilian level, that it was, somehow, the door itself telling him this. His heart pounded in his chest and his eyes rolled wide and staring as he approached the door. He no longer thought of his own danger, was no longer afraid of Nora's fate. He was moving forward now only for the door, for the *portal.*

It wanted him to open it, to pass through it into the beyond within. Under the heavy pull ring was a keyhole of preposterous size. The key to that door would have been massive, the size of a whiskey bottle or a pistol. Without it he could never hope to force a door of such blunt, awful strength.

His shaking hand reached out towards the door and it seemed his fingers only brushed it when the door unsealed and swung open under his touch like a dog coming to the hand of its master.

Then the door opened and things began to move too fast for Zach to question.

† † †

Zach stared into eternity.

Beyond the door an endless black canopy of space yawned out into distances too great for the mind to comprehend. Zach felt air rushing out of the Earth behind him into the trackless void. Stars were distant points of light spread out in successive, endless contours. Mute, Zach took in the vertiginous pan vista. He saw clusters of stars familiar from text books and television, but for which he'd never bothered to learn names.

Giddiness clutched him in an agoraphobic panic. He sagged against the rough-cut stone of the doorway, finally able to look away from the impossible and see the immediate. This was, in its own way, just as terrible as the voracious, infinite space all around him.

Before Zach a stone buttress arched into space, made of flagstone over massive granite slabs black with age. Horribly black with age. The walkway jutted out for nearly thirty meters before ending in a crumbling pie crust hanging out over nothing. Over nothing but stars like grains of sand and innumerable galaxies.

With sudden, terrifying realization, Zach saw that the ends of the arch were broken as if they had cracked and fallen away. He was staring at a bridge. A bridge, now broken, that had spanned out into that infinite and—

—suddenly, the potential of that was too huge, too alien, and his mind slid off the epiphany in an innate attempt to avoid madness.

Nora sobbed, secured to a pillar of stone rising up like a phallic insult. She saw Zach and screamed his name. Zach looked towards her and saw the figure coming towards him. He shrank back from the force of will he saw carved in stark, insane lines across an enraged face. Zach saw the heavy bladed knife the figure held and knew then what had laid his head open to the skull and taken his eye.

"You sonofabitch," Zach growled.

Before he was aware of what he was doing, he pushed away from the wall and started towards the approaching figure. Nora was screaming for him to help her, but, in this vast, open eternity the sound made it to Zach's ears as if she were calling across miles instead of merely scant meters.

The figure was on him. The man was tall, taller than Zach by at least head and shoulders, whipcord thin under the billowing, darkly purple robes. The face twisted with outrage and the left side of the *acolyte's* face was covered with a black eye patch under the robe's hood. A gold medallion hung from a thick chain around the man's neck, swinging furiously as he charged.

"Fool!" The acolyte screamed.

He lunged forward, heavy knife raised high overhead. Zach caught his arms as the man stabbed downwards. Zach gripped the acolyte's wrists, the blade pointing down at him like a fang. The man's strength was so terrible he seemed to fairly *thrum* with energy. Slowly, inexorably, the blade descended towards Zach's upturned face.

The man was craggy featured around a wide mouth twisting in hate and strain. The single eye in the man's face burned into Zach's own and seemed to radiate hate like heat.

"It comes fool!" The man hissed.

His words were nonsense to Zach. He was bent over under the man's strength until he thought his back would snap from the exertion and he was forced down onto his knees. The acolyte loomed above him, the point of the knife inches away.

Even as the acolyte tried to push his fat-bladed dagger into Zach's upturned face, he was talking. His bloodless, slash of a mouth elastic with horrible, frenzied whispers. He cursed Zach, mocked him, told him impossibilities.

This is all your fault! It wanted the girl; girl children feed it best. Give it a boy you idiot (in his panic Zach heard Big Ed's word 'idjit') *and it will come back sooner. Give it an adult and it will hardly sleep! Still, a woman is better than a man.*

Zach was pushed over and down onto the stones of the bridge. The acolyte straddled him in a horridly intimate movement. The tip of the knife was so close he knew he was moments from feeling cruel, unforgiving steel cut into him.

You think I'm bad you simple piece-of-shit? You think I'm evil? Fail to feed it and let it escape the portal! Cry for Babylon then, you imbecile!

Spittle flew from the man's mouth, striking Zach's face. Revulsion struck Zach in a tidal wave even stronger than his fear. He squirmed his head to one side to avoid more of the man's saliva. He felt the tip of the dagger gouge a furrow across his face but then, suddenly, his head was out from under the blade.

Zach whipped his face around and sank his teeth into the skeletal hands of the acolyte. He bit deep, the way a pit bull digs in, and he felt a salty, hot rush as blood squirted into his mouth. It was like drinking lava. The hooded, one-eyed acolyte screamed in pain and surprise.

He jerked his hand free from Zach's mouth, leaving behind a wad of flesh like chewing gum. The movement overextended the acolyte, and Zach—surging with new strength as if the man's blood were a fat line of coke like he sometimes used, but promised Nora he didn't—*pushed*.

He reached up and shoved the lanky man off him. The acolyte tumbled over as Zach spun on his back like some kid break-dancing down on South Beach. The acolyte snarled. Snarled like a dog, Zach thought, in a weirdly timeless pocket of perception before the man lifted his knife up and lunged.

Both of Zach's feet caught him flush in his face. They pistoned outwards, driving the acolyte up and back, carrying him smoothly over the edge of the broken bridge. Zach scrambled over to the ledge in disbelief.

The acolyte screamed as he fell and the scream stretched out between the two of them like a tether. The scream kept ringing in Zach's ears, even after the falling acolyte plummeted beyond the range of his vision.

Zach pushed himself shakily to his feet. The falling acolyte's message hadn't been one of rage; it had been a warning. Even as he was swallowed into the clutches of eternity, he had cried out to Zach in supplication. Pleaded with his killer to hear his warning.

It is coming.

Zach looked up. He saw Nora hysterical with relief. He made no move to free her. His eye slid off her the way his mind had slid off the idea of a bridge spanning eternity. Beyond her he looked out into the endless ocean of night. An ocean on which the race of man was no more than a mote in God's eye.

Zach felt icy cold running through him, and he knew in that moment. He knew but he still denied it to himself, the way he had denied every other shitty thing he'd ever done. But this time he's wasn't being selfish. Not this time.

Then, in the stretch of space, he saw it coming.

Nora still hadn't seen it and she screamed for him to untie her, to help her. *Give it an adult and it will hardly sleep! Still, a woman is better than a man.*

At first Zach saw only a hint of movement at the limits of his vision. He started towards Nora. He saw stars wink out then appear with each flap of tremendous wings.

You think I'm bad you simply piece of shit? You think I'm bad? Fail to feed it and let it escape the portal! Cry for Babylon then, you imbecile!

The memory of the acolyte's voice thundered in his head. Zach stopped, eyes locked to the endless space beyond Nora. Nora, who trusted him.

Give it an adult and it will hardly sleep! Still, a woman is better than a man.

Nora saw the mad fix of his stare and turned. She saw it coming, rising like a leviathan from antediluvian depths. She saw it and she began to scream for real. She turned back towards Zach, saw him motionless as a statue, the naked plea in her face crumpled as realization savaged her.

Zach turned and ran for the portal. He could hear the rasp of great, leathery wings behind him, felt the force of their beating. He made it to the door and yanked it open. He tumbled through the door as Nora uttered her final cry. It was long and piercing and anguished, and when he turned to close the door he met her eyes before the ancient thing ripped her head off her shoulders.

Without hesitation he slammed the door closed. For awhile he sat with his back hard up against the portal, trembling. But he didn't stay there for long. It was impossible because, though he heard Nora's scream echo in his head, the voice of the acolyte drowned her out.

Give it an adult and it will hardly sleep!

He had to find a little girl.

† † †† † †

So ends this night's
revels in the fields
of lost Arcadia
Goodnight sweet light,
vile dark,
blood moon
Until the gates
of Eternity
open
once more
adieu!

Adieu!

Deuce ex machina!